D1736103

The Secret Doctrine

of

The Rosicrucians

Illustrated with
The Secret Rosicrucian Symbols

MAGUS INCOGNITO

BARNES
&NOBLE
BOOKS
NEW YORK

This edition published by Barnes & Noble, Inc.

1993 Barnes & Noble Books

ISBN 1-56619-316-8
Printed and bound in the United States of America

M 9 8 7 6 5

TABLE OF CONTENTS

Female Universal Principle. Sex Manifest on All Planes of Existence. The Positive and the Negative Poles of Being. Sex Activity in Electricity and Magnetism. Sex, the Secret of Chemical Affinity. How Love Makes the World Go Round. How the One Becomes Two, and the Two Becomes the Many. ....Page 52

PART V

THE ONE AND THE MANY

How the One Becomes the Many. How Unity Becomes Diversity. How the Identical Becomes Variety. No Separation Possible to Unity. The Manifold Reflection of the One Reality. The Falling Raindrops. The Jars of Water. The Ocean of Being and Its Bubbles. Absolute Being Is One. Relative Being Is Apparently Many. Monism. Involution and Evolution. The World Soul and Its Material Garments. The Descent into Matter. The Ascent from Matter. The Spiral Stairway of Being. Sub-Mineral Forms. Mineral Forms. Plant Forms. Animal Forms. Human Forms. Superhuman Forms. God-like Forms. How the One Apparently Becomes Many, and Yet Remains One in Reality. The Paradox of Being..Page 62

PART VI

THE UNIVERSAL FLAME OF LIFE

The Sparks of the Flame of Life. The Rosicrucian Symbol of the Flaming Fire. The Fire of Spirit. The Essence of the Spiritual Flame of Life. Life Is Universal. There is Nothing Without Life in the Universe. The Universe Is Not Half-dead, but All-Alive. The Living Universe. Life in the Ether. Life in All Matter. The Universe a Living Dynamism. Life in the Atoms. Life in the Chemical Elements. Life in the Mineral World. Life in the Plant World. Life in the Animal World. Life in the Human World. Life in the Superhuman World. Life in the Divine World. Living Crystals. Scientific Proof of Life in the Inorganic World. Marvelous Reports of Modern Science. Metallic Vegetation. How Modern Science Confirms the Secret Doctrine of the Rosicrucians....Page 71

PART VII

THE PLANES OF CONSCIOUSNESS

The Seven Planes of Consciousness. Life the Essence of Spirit. Consciousness the Essence of Life. Everything Is Conscious. Nothing Is Unconscious. The Plane of Elemental Consciousness. Mental Action in the Atoms and Electrons. How the Occultist Works "Magic" by Knowledge of the Elemental Consciousness. The Plane of Mineral Consciousness. The Presence of Consciousness in the Crystals. The Secret of Cohesion and Mineral Organization. The Plane of Plant Consciousness. How Plants Manifest Intelligent Action. Plants Exhibit Consciousness Pertaining to Nutrition, Nervous Organization, and Thought Processes. Intelligence in Plants. Wonderful Reports of Modern Science. Rosicrucian Secret Doctrine Corroborated by Modern Science. The Plane of Animal Consciousness. The Evolution of Mind in the Animal World. A Fascinating Story. ....Page 85

PART VIII

THE THREE HIGHER PLANES OF CONSCIOUSNESS

The Plane of Human Consciousness. The Dawn of Self-Consciousness. The "I Am I." The Inward Mental Gaze. Simple Consciousness versus Self-Consciousness. The Psychology of Self-Consciousness. The Mystery of the Sense of Selfhood. How Man Pays the Price of Self-Consciousness. The Mastery of Mind. The Plane of the Consciousness of the Demi-Gods. The Light from Above. Mystic Experiences. Illumination. Cosmic Consciousness. At One with the Universe. Testimony of the Poets, Mystics, and Seers. Recognition of the Oversoul. The Phenomenon of Cosmic Consciousness. Beings Who Function Habitually on the Plane of the Demi-Gods. Legendary Beings of the Ancients. The Planes of the Consciousness of the Gods. Transcendental Knowledge. Exalted Beings "Like Unto the Gods." The Secret of the Archangels. The Truth of the Symbols. The Riddle of the Symbol..............................Page 117

PART IX

THE SEVENFOLD SOUL OF MAN

PART X

METEMPSYCHOSIS

PART XI

THE SOUL'S PROGRESS

PART XII

THE AURA AND THE AURIC COLORS

PART XIII

THE SEVEN COSMIC PRINCIPLES

The Secret Doctrine
of
The Rosicrucians

Figure 1. Mystic Symbol of the Rosicrucian Brotherhood

PART I

THE ROSICRUCIANS AND THEIR SECRET DOCTRINE

The student of the history of occultism and the esoteric teachings, and even the average reader of current books and magazines, finds many references to ''The Rosicrucians,'' a supposed ancient secret society devoted to the study of occult doctrines and the manifestation of occult powers. But when such person seeks to obtain detailed information concerning this supposed ancient ''order'' he finds himself baffled and defeated. Before acknowledging the futility of the quest, however, he usually investigates one or more so-called ''orders'' having as a part of their title the word ''Rosicrucian,'' only to find himself invited to join such ''order'' upon the payment of a fee or fees ranging from a small amount in some cases to quite large amounts in others, each ''order'' claiming to be the ''only original order,'' and asserting that all the others are base imitators.

The truth is that there is not in existence, and never has been in existence, any popular occult order sanctioned by the real Rosicrucians, which anyone may join upon payment of fees, large or small, just as he may join any of the better known fraternal organizations of which there are so many. The true Rosicrucians have no formal organization, and are held together only by the ties of common interest in the occult and esoteric studies, and by the common acceptance of certain fundamental principles of belief and knowledge. This unorganized ''order'' has members in all walks of life, and in all countries, and its members never announce themselves as ''Rosicrucians'' to the general public. Admission to this unorganized ''order'' is never granted upon the payment of a fee, and is possible only upon the request and recommendation of three members in good standing who have themselves been members for a certain period of time, and who have attained a certain degree of proficiency in the attainment of the esoteric knowledge, and in demonstrating the principles discovered by them under the direction of certain higher adepts in the arcane wisdom.

Members of the Rosicrucian body are prominent in the councils of nearly all of the occult organizations and societies throughout the world—in fact, it is these persons who are the real leaven in the general mass, and who keep alive the Sacred Flame of Truth in them. Many Rosicrucians are also prominent in philosophic and scientific circles, and some of them are men quite prominent in the large affairs of the business and professional world, and in the ranks of statesmanship. Others are prominent in movements like the ''labor movement'' and similar activities. Some are prominent in the councils of the various churches, and others are leaders in Masonry and similar secret societies. In all of such circles the Rosicrucians exert a powerful influence, and always in the direction of good.

''The Brothers of the Rosy Cross''

The modern interest in the Rosicrucian Teachings dates back to the early part of the seventeenth century—about 1610, to be exact. At that time there were rumors of the existence of a society known as "The Brothers of the Rosy Cross," the officers and meeting places of which were not known to the public. The mysterious society was severely attacked by the ecclesiastical authorities and others, and was as vigorously defended by those who were interested in the general subject of occultism and the esoteric teachings. There were many spurious and counterfeit "orders" established during the following century, and for that matter in nearly every century since, but none have been able to show an undoubted connection with the original order. Some of the original teachings of the Rosicrucians have been incorporated in some of the higher degrees of Masonry, and have served a good purpose therein.

The legend concerning the origin of the order—true in some respects, but erroneous in others—was as follows: That a certain Christian Rosenkreutz, a German nobleman who had donned the robes of a certain order of monks, had visited India, Persia, and also Arabia, and had returned bringing with him a certain Secret Doctrine obtained from the sages and seers of those Oriental lands. He was said to have established the original Rosicrucian Brotherhood about 1425, its existence not becoming generally known until nearly two hundred years afterward. The true Rosicrucians, however, recognize this legendary tale as being merely a cleverly disguised recital of the real facts of the establishment of the unorganized order, which must be read between the lines, aided by the spectacles of understanding, in order that its real import may be grasped.

The present writer does not feel justified in telling in these pages the tale as he understands it, and as it has been transmitted to him by those in authority; in fact, to make the same public, he would be violating a most sacred promise, which would amount to a betrayal of his initiation secrets. He, however, is permitted to state that the Secret Doctrine of the Rosicrucians is a body of esoteric teachings, handed down for ages by wise men deeply versed in the esoteric doctrines and occult lore. This Wisdom originally came by way of the Orient, and in fact even today comprises part of the Inner Teachings of some of the highest Oriental Brotherhoods. Its history is but another instance of the truth of the old Secret axioms, one of which says that we must "Look to the East, whence comes all Light."

For many years little or nothing was permitted to be revealed to the general public concerning the Secret Doctrine of the Rosicrucians, but during the past twenty-five years there has been a greater, and still greater freedom in this respect, until today many important Rosicrucian teachings form a part of nearly all writings and teachings upon the subject of the Esotericism in general, and of the Higher Metaphysics in particular. Theosophy, and the general interest in Oriental Philosophies and Religions, have done much to bring into public notice some of the more elementary points of the Secret Doctrine. In fact, in the highest writings and teachings of some of the great organizations above referred to the Rosicrucian may find many half-hidden bits of the Rosicrucian Doctrine, cleverly disguised from the unprepared Many, yet plainly revealed to the prepared Few.

The Higher Alchemy

The Rosicrucians, according to the public encyclopaedias, and other works of reference, are held to have been devoted to the subject of Alchemy. And, indeed, this statement is correct. But the modern compilers of such reference books have fallen into the error of supposing that the Alchemy referred to was performed wholly upon the Plane of Matter—and concerned wholly with the Transmutation of Elements. They are ignorant of the fact that the Alchemy which attracted the Rosicrucians, and which took up most of their time and attention, was Mental Alchemy, and Spiritual Alchemy—something quite different indeed, though having of course a correspondence to the Material Alchemy, according to the Law of Correspondence. The student of the present book will discover this fact, and will receive many valuable hints concerning the higher forms of Alchemy, providing he is prepared to read between the lines of the text, and to reason by Analogy. The axiom "As above, so below," will be found to work out well in this connection.

Why the Esoteric Teaching is Kept Secret

It is difficult to convey to the average European or American the true reasons underlying the Secrecy which invariably surrounds the Esoteric Teachings of all the great schools of occult thought. Such a person is inclined to think that the only reason therefor is the delight in "mystery mongering" which he thinks he finds among all occult teachers. But to one who penetrates even but a short distance on The Path, the true reasons are perceived. Such a one perceives the dangers of premature disclosure of important esoteric principles to the unprepared public mind. The following quotations from a well-known writer will perhaps give a hint to the solution of this question. The writer says:

"The Oriental method of cultivating knowledge has always differed diametrically from that pursued in the West during the growth of modern sciences. Whilst Europe has investigated Nature as publicly as possible, every step being discussed with the utmost freedom, and every fresh fact acquired circulated at once for the benefit of all, Asiatic science has been studied secretly and its conquests jealously guarded. I need not as yet attempt either criticism or defence of its methods. The student will later on see that this falls naturally into its place in the whole scheme of occult philosophy. The approaches to that philosophy have always been open, in one sense, to all. Vaguely throughout the world in various ways have been diffused the idea that some process of study which men here and there did actually follow, might lead to the acquisition of a higher kind of knowledge than that taught to mankind at large in books or by public teachers. The East, as pointed out, has always been more than vaguely impressed with this belief; but even in the West the whole block of symbolical literature relating to astrology, alchemy, and mysticism generally has fermented in European society, carrying to some peculiarly receptive and qualified minds the conviction that behind all this superficially meaningless nonsense great truths lay concealed. For such persons eccentric study has sometimes revealed hidden passages leading to the grandest imaginable realms of enlightenment. But till now, in all such cases, in accordance with the law of those schools, the neophyte no sooner forced his way into the region of mystery than he was bound over to the most inviolable secrecy as to everything connected with his entrance and further progress there. In Asia, in the same way, the chela, or pupil of occultism, no sooner became a chela than he ceased to be a witness on behalf of the reality of occult knowledge. I have been astonished to find, since my own connection with the subject, how numerous such chelas are. But it is impossible to imagine any human act more improbable than the unauthorized revelation by any such chela, to persons of the outer world, that he is one; and so the great esoteric school of philosophy successfully guards its seclusion. * * * It is however desirable to disabuse the reader of one conception in regard to the objects of adeptship that he very likely has formed. The development of those spiritual faculties, whose culture has to do with the highest objects of the occult life, gives rise as it progresses to a great deal of incidental knowledge, having to do with physical laws of Nature not yet generally understood. This knowledge, and the practical art of manipulating certain obscure forces of Nature, which it brings in its train, invest an adept, and even an adept's pupils, at a comparatively early stage of their education, with very extraordinary powers, the application of which to matters of daily life will sometimes produce results that seem altogether miraculous; and from the ordinary point of view, the acquisition of apparently miraculous power is such a stupendous achievement, that people are sometimes apt to fancy that the adept's object in seeking the knowledge he attains has been to invest himself with these coveted powers. It would be as reasonable to say of any great patriot of military history that his object in becoming a soldier has been to wear a gay uniform and impress the imagination of the nurse maids.''

"The Secret Doctrine of the Rosicrucians"

What is known as "The Secret Doctrine of the Rosicrucians" is an extensive body of esoteric teaching and occult lore which has been transmitted from Master to Student, from Hierophant to the new Initiate, for countless generations. Seldom has any part of the Secret Doctrine been committed to writing, or exposed to public view on the printed page, until the present generation. Previous to that time the little that was written, or printed, concerning this body of teachings was disguised in the vague terms of alchemy and astrology, so that the same would have one meaning to the average reader and another and closer meaning to those who possessed the key to the mystery. The frequent references in the ancient books to "sulphur," "mercury," and other chemical elements, and to "The Philosopher's Stone," etc., were all intended to indicate certain portions of the teachings of the Secret Doctrine to those who already possessed the key.

The Secret Doctrine of the Rosicrucians is believed by those best informed to have been built up gradually, carefully, and slowly, by the old occult masters and adepts, from the scattered fragments of the esoteric teachings which were treasured by the wise men of all races. The legend runs that these fragments of the Secret Doctrine were the scattered portions of the old esoteric teaching of ancient Atlantis —the bits of the great mass of the Atlantean occult teachings which were scattered in all directions by the great cataclysm which had destroyed that great continent. The few survivors of the Atlantean civilization carefully preserved these Fragments of Truth, and passed them on to their chosen students and capable descendants.

The old Masters who made it the object of their
lives to gather together once more these scattered
fragments, and to thus reconstruct the Occult Doctrine of the Atlanteans, found a portion of their material in Egypt, in India, in Persia, in Chaldea, in
Medea, in China, in Assyria, and in Ancient Greece,
and also in the mystic records of the Hebrews, such
as the Kaballah and the Zohar. The common source,
however, may be regarded as distinctly Oriental.
The great philosophies of the East, in fact, may be
said to have been built upon the base of these still
more ancient teachings. Moreover, the great Grecian Secret Teachings are believed to have been
based upon knowledge obtained from this same common source. So, at the last, the Secret Doctrine of
the Rosicrucians may be said to be the Secret Doctrine of Atlantis, transmitted through the descendants of the people of that great centre of occult
knowledge.

The following quotation from a writer who, himself, has gathered together many bits of the ancient
wisdom, may be interesting. Speaking of these ancient teachings he says: ''The teaching has come
down to the present age through the corridors of
time, from the dim ages of past eras, races, and
schools of thought. Even those highest in the ancient occult councils, however, are unable to trace
the teachings, in an unbroken direct line, further
back than the time of Pythagoras (about 500 B. C.),
and a little later in Ancient Greece, although they
find many references thereto, and extracts therefrom, in some of the older records of ancient Egypt
and Chaldea, which serve to show that the schools of
Pythagoras, and other ancient Grecian occultists,
were founded on occult instruction still more remote,

received in a direct line of succession of teachers and pupils extending over centuries. Investigators have found traces of the teachings in the records of Persia and Media, and it is believed that the inspiration for the original philosophical teachings of Gautama, the founder of Buddhism, was received from the same sources. Traces are also found in the Hebrew Esoteric Teachings.''

The writer continues: ''The Grecian Teachings were undoubtedly obtained directly from Egyptian sources, through Pythagoras, the relation between the early Grecian teachings and philosophies, and the older school of old Egypt, being very close and intimate. Pythagoras is known to have received instruction from Egyptian and Persian hierophants. There is to be found the closest resemblance between the ancient Grecian teachings, and those of the Egyptian Esoteric Fraternities. Some of the Teachers, however, hold that the Grecian and Egyptian schools, respectively, were but two separate offshoots of an original and older Teaching which had its origin in the lost continent of Atlantis. There are many traditions connecting the Teaching with Atlantis, and it is possible that both Greece and Egypt received it from this common source, instead of Greece being indebted to Egypt for the line of transmission. But, be this as it may, it is a fact that all of the traces of teaching that the various occultists gather from the traditions, scraps of doctrine, and legends regarding Atlantis, can be reconciled with the best esoteric and occult knowledge had by the race today. The fragments of the Egyptian Esoteric Teachings, many of which are still preserved in an undoubted direct line of succession, are practically identical, in fundamental and basis points, with the Grecian Occult Teachings. And, as has been said, the Persian, Medean, and Chaldean legends and traditions, and scraps of teachings which have been preserved, show a common source or origin with those of Egypt and ancient Greece."

The writer adds: "We are speaking now of the historical view of the subject, only. The occult traditions hold that the Teaching, in some form, is as old as the race itself, and has been known to the advanced minds of every great civilization of the past, many of which disappeared thousands of years ago, all traces of them having been lost to the present sub-race. The traditions hold that the Teaching was handed down from the Elder Brethren of the race—certain advanced souls who appeared in the earlier days, in order to plant the seeds of Truth, so that they would grow, blossom, and bear fruit throughout the ages to follow. We do not ask you to accept this statement—it is not material—for the Teaching bears evidences of its own Truth within itself, without needing the force of such high authority. The ancient tradition is mentioned merely that the student may know that the same is accepted as truth by many of the highest occult authorities and teachers."

"The Seven Aphorisms of Creation"

In the present book, the writer has presented for the consideration of his readers "The Seven Aphorisms of Creation" of the Rosicrucians, which embody the fundamental principles of the Rosicrucian Secret Doctrine. He has also reproduced the leading Secret Symbols of the Rosicrucians which relate to the Seven Aphorisms of Creation.

The student who will master the principles herein

set forth will have brought himself to a plane of thought which will naturally tend to place him en rapport with the higher teachers of the Rosicrucians, and to render him subject to the offer of still higher information should he desire to proceed further into this great study. Let the student always remember the ancient axiom: "When the Pupil is ready, the Master appears." But the Pupil is not "ready" until he has **mastered** the elementary instruction such as is given in the pages of this book.

It is not claimed, however, that in the pages of this book are given **all** the Secret Teachings of the Rosicrucians, such as their Formulas and Methods of Mental Alchemy, and Spiritual Transmutation. Such information cannot be cast broadcast, for reasons which will be apparent to every earnest and intelligent student. But, on the other hand, **such information cannot be withheld from those who are ready to receive it,** and who are moved by the proper motives in seeking to acquire the secret knowledge. When the student learns how to give "The Right Knock," then will he find proven the old promise: "Knock, and it shall be opened unto you."

The Symbol of the Rosy Cross

The well-known Symbol of the Rosicrucians— "The Rosy Cross"—appears in several forms, as for instance: The Cross surmounted by the Rose; the Sword (the Cross handle) attached to the Rose; the Cross surmounted by the Crown; a modification of the Phallic Cross, etc. The explanation of the general Symbol is Sevenfold—the three highest being reserved for Initiates of a certain rank, only, and therefore cannot be stated here. Below follow several

of the meanings which we are permitted to translate
and explain here:

(1) **The Cross Surmounted by the Rose**, indicates
that the "Rose" (the mystic symbol of the Divine)
can be attained only by the suffering of mortal life
(symbolized by the Cross).

Figure 2. The Symbol of the Rosy Cross. (Conventionalized)

(2) **The Sword Attached to the Rose** indicates that
the Sword of the Spirit must be actively employed
in the Battle of Life, in order to win the reward of
the Rose (the Rose being the reward bestowed by
the Queen upon the victorious Knight, in the olden
days).

(3) **The Cross Surmounted by the Crown**, indicates that the suffering of mortal existence, borne
by the faithful disciple of Truth, will inevitably be
rewarded by the attainment of the Crown of Mastery.
"Every Cross has its Crown"; and "No Cross, no

Crown''; being old aphorisms seeking to express this truth.

(4) The Modified Phallic Cross, indicates the Sexual Duality of the Manifested Universe—the Presence and Activity of the Universal Male Principle and the Universal Female Principle, respectively. [The Modified Phallic Cross of the Rosicrucians, however, must not be taken to indicate any relationship of the Rosicrucians with the gross forms of Phallic Worship, however. The latter is merely the distorted shadow of the Truth, and must not be mistaken for the Reality.]

Concluding this introductory statement, and inviting you to enter into the study of the Secret Doctrine of the Rosicrucians, let us ask you to carefully consider the following words of an ancient aphorism: ''The possession of Knowledge, unaccompanied by a manifestation and expression in Action, is like the hoarding of precious metals by the miser—a vain and foolish thing. Forget not The Law of Use, in this and all other things.''

PART II

THE ETERNAL PARENT

In the Secret Doctrine of the Rosicrucians we find the following Aphorism of Creation:

The First Aphorism

I. The Eternal Parent was wrapped in the Sleep of the Cosmic Night. Light there was not: for the Flame of Spirit was not yet rekindled. Time there was not: for Change had not re-begun. Things there were not: for Form had not re-presented itself. Action there was not: for there were no Things to act. The Pairs of Opposites there were not: for there were no Things to manifest Polarity. The Eternal Parent, causeless, indivisible, changeless, infinite, rested in unconscious, dreamless sleep. Other than the Eternal Parent there was Naught, either Real or Apparent.

In this First Aphorism of Creation the Rosicrucian student is directed to apply his attention to the concept of the Infinite Source of All Things—the Eternal Parent "from which all things proceed." This Eternal Parent—the Infinite Unmanifest, is represented by the Rosicrucians by the symbol of a circle, having nothing outside of itself and nothing within itself.

The circle, however, must not be interpreted as conveying the idea of limitation; rather is it intended to convey the idea of limitlessness. The symbol, although the best possible for the purpose, is inadequate—this by reason of the impossibility of representing the Infinite by a finite symbol. The only adequate symbol of the Eternal Parent would be that of Infinite Space, and this, of course, cannot be represented by a sign, for no matter how wide the circle might be drawn there would always be Space beyond it. But, recognizing the impossibility of an

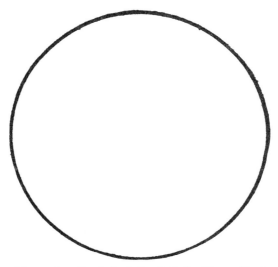

Figure 3.   Symbol of the Infinite Unmanifest

adequate symbol, the ancient Rosicrucians have adopted the empty circle as the best possible finite symbol of the Infinite Unmanifest.

The concept of Infinite Space has always been regarded by the Rosicrucians as the best possible concept with which to "think of" the Infinite Unmanifest, since the latter cannot be actually "thought" in consciousness as a Thing, and consciousness is capable of thinking only of Things. Strictly speaking, the Infinite Unmanifest is a "Nothing" rather than a "Thing"; and yet not such a "Nothing" as implies "not-ness" or "naught," but rather such a "Nothing" as implies "The Possibility of Everything, yet without the limitations of Thingness."

Infinite Space cannot be considered a "Thing," for it has none of the characteristics of a "Thing." And yet it cannot be denied actual existence and presence. Roughly speaking, it may be defined as "A No-Thing, containing within itself the possibility of infinite Thingness, or the infinite possibility of Things." Infinite Space must be thought of as the Absolute Container of Everything, whether Manifest or Unmanifest—for outside of Infinite Space there is only Nothingness, or, more strictly speaking, there is no **outside** of Infinite Space.

Infinite Space, therefore, has always been the accepted occult and esoteric symbol by means of which men are able to "think of" the Infinite Unmanifest—the Eternal Parent, wrapped in the Sleep of the Cosmic Night. In one of the ancient occult catechisms, the question was asked: **"What is that which ever has been, is now, and ever shall be, whether there be a Universe or not, and whether there be gods or not?"** And the answer is: **"Space!"**

The strength of this symbol of Infinite Space, as indicating the Infinite Unmanifest, is perceived when the mind tries to think, or even imagine, the absence of Infinite Space—either as absent before its creation, or else as absent after its destruction. It will, of course, be discovered that the human mind, and the human imagination, finds it impossible to think of Space being absent in either event. The mind is compelled to think of Space as being Infinite, and as being Eternal, without regard to whatever else is held to be either present or absent at any time, past, present, or future. And at the same time, the mind finds that it is unable to define Space as a Thing—yet it dare not regard it as a Nothing or Naught. It is found that Infinite Space must be always thought of as necessarily eternally present, and yet ever free from the limitations of Things.

Moreover, as Infinite Space is invisible and beyond the other senses, it cannot be "known" or cognized as a Thing. Thought regarding it must always report "not this; not that" regarding it; and it answers to the ancient sage's statement of Reality that: "The Essence of Being is without attributes, formless, devoid of distinctions, and unconditioned. It is different from that which we know, and from that which we do not know. Words and thought turn from it without finding it. The wise answer only by silence all questions concerning its nature. To all suggestions concerning its qualities, properties, and attributes, the wise simply answer: 'neti, neti'—'not this, not that!' Of THAT the wise assert simply 'It IS.'" And as other ancient sages have said: "The imagination, the understanding, and abstract thinking will always strive in vain to represent the Infinite; for no form of finiteness (to which thought and speech also belong) can express the Infinite; nor can that which was timed express the Timeless and Eternal; nor can thought resultant from the chain of causation grasp the Causeless or Self-Existent." So, in every way, and from every angle of view, we discover that the concept of Infinite Space is a noble and worthy symbol of THAT which we mean when we try to think of the Infinite Unmanifest—of the Essence of Being before Manifestation into Activity and Form.

The First Aphorism states that **"The Eternal**

Parent was wrapped in the Sleep of the Cosmic Night.''

In this sentence there is a reference to that teaching concerning the Cosmic Days and Nights, which under some of many names is found lying at the base of all esoteric teachings and occult philosophies. The highest human and superhuman intelligences have testified to the fact that Rhythm is abiding in, and manifest through, the Cosmos—from the tiniest point of Manifested Being to the Totality of Being, there is found to ever exist the presence and manifestation of Rhythm.

There is reported to us from the highest occult sources of information the fact that the ALL presents Itself alternately in great periods of Manifestation (called the Cosmic Days), followed by a like great period of Unmanifestation (called the Cosmic Nights). During the Cosmic Night the Eternal Parent exists as if wrapped in an unconscious and dreamless sleep, from which with the Dawn of the new Cosmic Day it awakens gradually into Manifestation. The Cosmic Day, in turn, gradually finds itself changing into a Twilight, which slowly but surely darkens into the Cosmic Night when all again is stilled and quiet. And so on, and on, and on, in infinite sequence and repetition—in infinite rhythm— the Cosmos presents this succession of Days and Nights: of Manifestation and Unmanifestation. And, so it has been forever and ever, and will continue forever and ever, without end, ceasing, or interruption. Such is the report of the wise and the illumined teachers of the race.

A great occult teacher has written of this teaching, as follows: ''The Esoteric Doctrine teaches, like Buddhism and Brahmanism, and even the Kabala, that the one infinite and unknown Essence exists from all eternity, and in regular and harmonious successions is either passive or active. In the poetical phraseology of Manu these conditions are called the 'Days' and the 'Nights' of Brahma. The latter is either 'awake' or 'asleep' * * * Upon inaugurating an active period, says the Secret Doctrine, an expansion of this Divine Essence from without inwardly, and from within outwardly, occurs in obedience to eternal and immutable law, and the phenomenal or visible universe is the ultimate result of the long chain of cosmical forces thus progressively set in motion. In like manner, when the passive condition is resumed, a contraction of the Divine Essence takes place, and the previous work of creation is gradually and progressively undone. The visible universe becomes disintegrated, its material dispersed, and 'darkness' solitary and alone, broods once more over the face of the 'deep.' To use a metaphor from the Secret Books, which will convey the idea more clearly, an out-breathing of the 'unknown essence' produces the world; and an inhalation causes it to disappear. This process has been going on from all eternity, and our present universe is but one of an infinite series, which had no beginning and will have no end."

In this connection, the student of Herbert Spencer will find in the ancient occult doctrines and teachings an unsuspected firm basis for the teaching of his modern master. Spencer in his teaching of the universal presence and activity of Rhythm but echoes the old occult teachings on the subject. Note the following from the pen of the modern prophet of Evolution: "Apparently, the universally co-existent forces of attraction and repulsion which, as we have seen, necessitate rhythm in all minor changes throughout the universe, also necessitate rhythm in the totality of its changes—produce now an immeasurable period during which the attracting forces predominating, cause universal concentration, and then an immeasurable period, during which the repulsive forces predominating, cause universal diffusion—alternate eras of Evolution and Dissolution.''

The First Aphorism further states: "**Light there was not: for the Flame of Spirit was not yet rekindled.''**

This is apt to prove a "hard saying" to those who, having the half-truth only, and not realizing the existence of the other half, have thought of Infinite Reality as being Spirit, of which the Flame is of course the occult and esoteric symbol. But the best ancient wisdom, as voiced by the most careful teachers, have ever taught those qualified to know the whole truth that not only back of Matter, but also back of Spirit, there abides an Eternal and Infinite Essence, which is neither Spirit nor Matter, but which is the unconditioned root and source of both Spirit and Matter. Light and Flame—the two universally recognized esoteric and occult symbols of Spirit—have back of them the "lightless and heatless" Essence of Light and Heat. The Infinite Reality is the Essence of the Spirit Light and Flame —not the Light and Flame itself. The student will be aided in grasping this truth, if he will contemplate the flame of a lamp, a candle, a gas-flame, or any other kind of physical flame; he will perceive to be present, under and at the centre of the flame, a dark, transparent, "something" which is the "essence" from which the Flame itself proceeds, and upon which it draws for support and sustenance. In occult terminology the counterpart of this on the higher planes of Being is called "the Dark Flame"—it is the Essence of the Flame and Light, and not Flame or Light itself. As an ancient writer has said: "The Essence is the 'spirit of the fire,' and not Fire itself; therefore, the attributes of Fire, i. e., heat, flame, and light, are not the attributes of the Essence, but rather of the Fire of which the Essence is the Cause."

Therefore, the Infinite Unmanifest—the sleeping Eternal Parent—must not be thought of by the student as being Spirit, in the sense of the latter term as commonly employed in our thought. Rather is it akin to Pure Space from which the Flame emerges, and in which it is contained. There is close reasoning and distinction here, which will become clear to the student as he proceeds, but which must be noted even now in passing.

The First Aphorism further states: **"Time there was not: for Change had not begun."**

Here, again, is expressed another "hard saying" for the student who has not grasped the true meaning of "Time." Time, in the strict philosophical meaning of the term, does not mean **pure duration of existence**—instead, it means "the measure of changing existence." An enduring existence in which there is no change of form, activity, or degree, mental or physical, is Timeless. Time, in fact, is but the "measure of Change." Without Change there can be no Time, in the true sense of the latter term. Pure Being manifests not Time. Time is the result of Becoming, or Change, and is always measured by change or becoming in something.

The following statement from a modern text book may serve to point to the difference between the conception of Pure Duration, and Time: "Pure Duration is conceived without regard to the motions of changes in things. Time on the contrary is the sensible measure of any portion of duration, often marked by particular phenomena, as the apparent revolution of the celestial bodies, the rotation of the earth on its axis, etc. Our conception of Time originates in that of motions; and particularly in those regular and equable motions carried on in the heavens, the parts of which, from their perfect similarity to each other, are correct measures of the continuous and successive quantity called Time, with which they are conceived to co-exist. Time, therefore, may be defined as, 'The perceived number of successive movements. Time, based upon the movements of the celestial bodies, or the earth, is frequently measured by instruments based upon such movements, such as watches, clocks, sun-dials, etc."

We are also conscious of the passage of Time by changes in our mental states, our thoughts, our mental images, etc., both in the waking state or the state of dreams. Without changes in the outside world, represented to our consciousness by perceptions of such changes, or without changes in our mental states, Time would not exist for us. It thus follows that given an Eternal Changeless Reality, for whom and by whom no "outside world" has been or is manifested; and which is wrapped in an unconscious and dreamless sleep, such as is pictured in the First Aphorism; for such a Reality there could exist no Time—no Time would present itself—Timelessness would abide, until Change began once more.

Therefore, the student will perceive the necessary truth of the statement of the First Aphorism that for the Eternal Parent, wrapped in the Sleep of the Cosmic Night, "Time there was not: for Change had not begun.'' It is impossible to hold otherwise, considering the nature of Time, and the absence of Change during the Cosmic Night of the Eternal Parent. The student will perceive that given Infinite Existence, and the absence of Change, then we must necessarily postulate Pure Duration, and the absence of Time. There is no logical escape from this conclusion.

The First Aphorism further states: **"Things there were not: for Form had not re-presented itself."**

Here, again, we are presented with an unescapable conviction. A ''Thing'' is ''Whatever exists, or is conceived to exist, as a separate entity, and as a separable or distinguishable object of thought.'' Every ''Thing'' must manifest ''form.'' ''Form'' is (1) the shape or structure of anything, as distinguished from the material of which it is composed, hence, the configuration or figure of anything; (2) the mode of acting or manifestation of anything to the senses, or to the intellect; (3) the assemblage of qualities constituting a conception, or the internal constitution making an existing thing what it is.''

Strictly speaking a ''Thing'' must be capable of being thought of or pictured as composed of qualities, attributes, or properties distinguishing it from other things; hence every ''Thing'' must manifest form in order to be so distinguished and perceived by the senses or by the intellect as a Thing. The Eternal Parent—the Infinite Unmanifest—cannot be held to manifest Form, or to display or present any particular quality, property, or attribute of Manifestation, when in its state of Unmanifestation. When the Eternal Parent takes upon itself the robes of Manifestation it proceeds to manifest the appearance of Things—these Things each displaying Form, and certain qualities, properties, or attributes which distinguish them from other manifested Things. It it axiomatic in metaphysics and philosophy that the Unmanifest cannot be thought of as possessing or manifesting (in its essential nature) any one set of qualities, properties, or attributes which appear later in its Manifestation of Things, as distinguished from the opposite set of qualities, properties, or attributes. And it cannot be thought of as possessing (in its essential nature) of both of the opposing sets of qualities, attributes, or properties, for "opposites cancel each other," and "antinomies condition not."

Instead of possessing qualities, properties, or attributes—or Form, in any of the meaning of that term—the Unmanifest must be regarded as possessing the "possibility of infinite manifestation of Form, qualities, properties, and attributes in its manifestations," or "the infinite possibility of the manifestation of Form, qualities, properties, or attributes in its manifested Things." The Infinite Unmanifest cannot be thought of as a Thing, either in itself, or by means of its symbol of Infinite Space. Rather, as an illumined occult master has expressed it, it must be regarded as "An Omnipresent, Eternal, Boundless, and Immutable **Principle**, regarding which all speculation is impossible, since it transcends the power of human conception and could only be dwarfed by any human expression or similitude. It is beyond the range and reach of thought—it is unthinkable and unspeakable."

In the period of the Cosmic Night, there being nothing present except the Infinite Unmanifest, therefore it is seen that, necessarily, "Things there were not: for Form had not re-presented itself." There is no logical escape from this conclusion.

The First Aphorism further states: "**Action there was not: for there were no Things to act.**"

This statement requires little or no explanation. There being no Things present, there were no Things to act. And all action of the Infinite must be through, by, or in Things. All action requires Change, and where there is no Change there can be no action. And yet, it must not be thought that the Infinite Unmanifest is powerless, for it possesses all Power; it must not be thought that it is motionless, for in itself it is Abstract Motion. Speaking in finite terms, it may be said that in its state of the Infinite Unmanifest the Eternal Parent dwells in a state of such infinite Motion that as compared with relative Motion it is in a state of Absolute Rest.

The First Aphorism further states: "**The Pairs of Opposites there were not: for there were no Things to manifest Polarity.**"

As every student of philosophy knows, or should know, every Thing manifests a combination of qualities, properties, or attributes. Each quality, property, or attribute, is one of a Pair of Opposites—one Pole of the Two Poles of Qualities which are ever found present. Given one quality, property, or attribute of Thingness, it necessarily follows that there is in existence in other Things an Opposite, or "Other Pole"—its antithesis. There is no exception to this rule, and though the Opposite may at first appear to be absent, diligent search will surely reveal it, and its necessary existence must be logically predicated.

Thus we have the following familiar Opposites: Hard and Soft, Hot and Cold, Large and Small, Far and Near, Up and Down, Day and Night, Light and Darkness, Long and Short, etc. Even where our language fails to supply a definite term for the Opposite of a discovered quality, property, or attribute, the Opposite may be expressed by prefixing the term "Not" to the observed quality, property, or attribute.

Some thinkers have sought to imply that the term "Infinite" implies a quality, property, or attribute which was the opposite of Finite, but this is merely a play upon words. The word "Infinite" implies simply **an absence of limitations, bounds, or form,** and does not indicate any limit, bound, or form no matter how extended. It is impossible to form a mental image of The Infinite Unmanifest, or to attach Thingness or Form, or quality, property, or attribute of any kind to it—hence the term "Infinity" is not a true Opposite. It is only when Manifestation begins that the Pairs of Opposites or Polarity put in an appearance.

The Infinite Unmanifest possesses the possibility of an infinity of manifestations, all objects of which manifestation must exhibit one or the other of any given set of qualities, properties, or attributes. But to the Infinite Unmanifest itself—the Eternal Parent, in its essence—there can be no Polarity or presence of any one set of Pairs of Opposites.

Here, as elsewhere, the student is directed to think of the Infinite Unmanifest by means of its symbol of Infinite Space, whenever he wishes to test any of the statements of the First Aphorism.

The First Aphorism finally states: **"The Eternal Parent, causeless, indivisible, changeless, infinite, rested in unconscious, dreamless, sleep. Other than the Eternal Parent there was Naught, either Real or Apparent."**

That the Eternal Parent is Causeless is a self-evident fact, for there is nothing which could have caused the Eternal and Original Being, from which all Manifestation proceeds. That which is Eternal must, of necessity, be Causeless. That which is Infinite, can have no Other which could have caused it. And it could not have been caused from or by Nothing, for "from Nothing, nothing comes."

That the Eternal Parent is Indivisible is likewise self-evident, for anything that can be divided or separated into parts or particles, must in the first place be originally composed of parts or particles. And anything that is composed of parts or particles must be merely a Composition, an Aggregate, a Collection, or Crowd of such parts and particles, and, therefore, not a Real Entity or Unity at all. Moreover, that which is Infinite cannot become divided or separated into parts or particles without losing its essential Infinity—a divided Infinite is no Infinite at all, but merely a Collection or Crowd of Finite Things. Absolute Indivisibility must be predicated of True Unity and Infinite Being. There is no logical escape from this conclusion.

That the Eternal Parent is incapable of Essential Change is likewise self-evident, for though It may manifest an infinity of change, nevertheless it must always remain essentially Itself, and never anything else but Itself. Moreover, not being composed essentially of qualities, properties, or attributes, it cannot undergo the change which comes from the shifting of the poles of the Opposites. And not having Form, it cannot experience the change which arises from Change of Form. Absolute Immutability must be predicated of the Eternal Parent. There is no logical escape from this conclusion.

That the Eternal Parent is Infinite is likewise self-evident. It must be Infinite, for there is nothing else by which it may be limited, defined, bounded, caused, influenced, or affected. That which is Absolute and Original, Ultimate and Elementary, can have no binding or limiting conditions or Things. Absolute Infiniteness must be predicated of the Eternal Parent. There is no logical escape from this conclusion.

That the Eternal Parent rested in "Unconscious, dreamless sleep" is held by all advanced metaphysicians and philosophers to be a logical necessity, if we are to postulate the existence of a period or state of Unmanifestation. For, as all psychologists and philosophers know, consciousness (even in the form of dreams) is impossible without Change. A changeless state of consciousness can only be expressed as Unconsciousness. And yet, the student must not fall into the error of believing that this Infinite Unconsciousness implies "inferiority to consciousness"; for rather does it imply a state of "rising above" ordinary consciousness—a state of Infinite Super-Consciousness—a state of transcending consciousness, in which there is ever present the "possibility of consciousness" without the exercise thereof. Ordinary consciousness is a **descent** from this state of Unconsciousness, not an **ascent**. This distinction is important, and must not be lost sight of by the student.

As we shall presently discover, when Manifestation begins to dawn into appearance, then, and then only, the Eternal Parent may be said to begin to "dream"—to dream of an infinity of universes, succeeding each other in rhythmic sequence. And only when the Eternal Parent shall awaken fully from the dream, into the bright noon-tide of infinite self-consciousness, may It be thought of as being fully "awake" and conscious. These facts will unfold themselves as we proceed with the consideration of the Aphorisms.

"**Other than the Eternal Parent there was Naught, either Real or Apparent.**" Here, again, we have a self-evident truth. There can have been no other Real being—no "other" to the Infinite and Absolute Reality—for the predicate of Infinity and Absoluteness carries with it the implicit predicate of Aloneness, Oneness, and Uniqueness. There can be no "other" Real being to Infinite Reality. And, in the absence of Manifestation, there can have been no Apparent (i. e., manifested or "created" Thing or Things) Thing in existence in the period of the Infinite Unmanifestation. There is no logical escape from this conclusion.

Finally, the student is once more bidden to fall back upon the symbol of Infinite Space, in this consideration of the Infinite Unmanifest, whenever he finds it difficult, or almost impossible, to conceive of the truth of the statements contained in the First Aphorism as concerned with the Eternal Parent in the state of the Infinite Unmanifest, in the Cosmic Night. The symbol will be found perfectly adequate in order to permit one to "think of the Infinite Unmanifest," although, of course, it is impossible to paint a mental picture of either symbol or the reality which it represents.

Edgar Allen Poe has well said of the thought and concept of "The Infinite," and similar efforts of the human mind to think of the unthinkable: "This merest of words, and some other expressions of which the equivalents exist in nearly all languages, is by no means the expression of an idea, but of an effort of one. It stands for the possible attempt at an impossible conception. Man needed a term by which to point out the **direction** of this effort—the cloud behind which lay, forever invisible, the **object** of this attempt. A word, in fine, was demanded by means of which one human being might put himself in relation at once with another human being and with a certain **tendency** of the human intellect. Out of this arose this term, which is thus the representative but of **the thought of a thought.** * * * The fact is that, upon the enunciation of any one of that class of terms to which this belongs,—the class representing **thoughts of thought,**—he who has a right to say that he thinks **at all** feels himself called upon **not** to entertain a conception, but simply to direct his mental vision toward some given point in the intellectual firmament where lies a nebula never to be solved. To solve it, indeed, he makes no effort, for with a rapid instinct he comprehends, not only the impossibility, but as regards all human purposes, the inessentiality of its solution. He sees at once how it lies **out** of the brain of man, and even **how,** if not exactly **why,** it lies out of it.''

In the Secret Doctrine of the Rosicrucians, therefore, there is no attempt made to **define** the Essence of the Eternal Parent—in fact, it is held, in the spirit of Spinoza's celebrated aphorism, that "To **define** The Infinite is to **deny** The Infinite.'' In refusing to ascribe the finite qualities, properties, and attributes of Personality to the Eternal Parent, the Rosicrucians do not mean to imply that The Infinite Reality is **below** the plane of Personality, but rather that **it** is so immeasurably **above** that plane, and so infinitely transcends all Personality, that it is childish to think or speak of it in the terms of Personality.

It has been held by eminent thinkers that even the

finite intelligence of man is capable of conceiving of a state of intelligence as much higher than that of the most intelligent man as the latter is higher than that of the black beetle. This being so, it can readily be seen that such a Power, to which the manifestation of such a superlative degree of intelligence being is but a bagatelle effort of power, is, and must be, in its essential nature so infinitely above the plane of human personality that it is practically an insult to think of it in the terms of Personality.

As has been frequently stated in this consideration of the First Aphorism, the state of Being of the Infinite and Absolute Reality—the Eternal Parent—during this state of the Infinite Unmanifest cannot be expressed in words, for it is beyond words. It can be thought of only symbolically—by means of Its only possible symbol, i. e., that of Infinite Space. Even symbolized, it can be thought of only in terms of negation; for being in the state of Absolute Being (which as Hegel says is practically identical with Non-Being, when the term "Being" is used in the sense of finite, conditioned, and qualified Being), it cannot be thought of as possessing any of the qualities, attributes, or properties of Thingness. Therefore, its state of Being can be suggested only by using the terms implying the negation of all those qualities, properties, and attributes which men ascribe to Things—even to those Things which they feel rather than conceive, and which represent even the remotest limits of their mentative efforts.

Edwin Arnold, in his beautiful poem "The Light of Asia," has well expressed the Buddhistic conception of this "beyond-thoughtness" of the Essence of the Infinite Reality, in the following words:

"Om Amataya! Measure not with words the Immeasurable;
Nor sink the string of thought into the Fathomless.
Who asks does err; who answers, errs; say naught!
Shall any gazer see with mortal eyes?
Or any searcher know with mortal mind?
Veil after veil will lift—but there must be
Veil upon veil behind!"

And, so, the Rosicrucians regard the fact of the Infinite Unmanifest—the Absolute Essence—only under the symbol of the Infinite Sea of Pure Space, resting in a state of Absolute Calm and Absolute Transparency through which the mortal eye gazes and seems to see but NOTHING: but which the Illumined Intuition knowness to be Allness instead of Nothingness—Absolute and Infinite Being instead of Nothingness—Infinite Life, instead of Death!

Though it cannot be perceived by mortal sense, and though it transcends the highest effort of both intellect and imagination to conceive or picture, yet the highest reports of Pure Reason inform us that it must be present, and the highest reports of Intuitive Faith render it impossible to doubt its all-presence and reality. To the ignorant and the half-wise, this symbol may seem to indicate Nothing: but to the illumined and truly wise, it is seen to represent Absolute ALLNESS of Reality. Gaze ye, then, upon this symbol of Infinite Space with awe, for it represents our highest (though feeble) efforts at expressing the nature of the Infinite Essence of Being!

PART III

THE SOUL OF THE WORLD

In the Secret Doctrine of the Rosicrucians we find the following Second Aphorism:

The Second Aphorism

II. The Germ within the Cosmic Egg takes unto itself Form. The Flame is re-kindled. Time begins. A Thing exists. Action begins. The Pairs of Opposites spring into being. The World Soul is born, and awakens into manifestation. The first rays of the new Cosmic Day break over the horizon.

In this Second Aphorism of Creation the Rosicrucian is directed to apply his attention to the concept of the World Soul—the First Manifestation of the Eternal Parent. This World Soul—the First Manifestation—is represented by the Rosicrucians by the symbol of a circle containing at its centre a black dot or point. The circle, of course, represents the Infinite Unmanifest, and the black dot or point represents the Focal Point of the new Manifestation—the "Germ within the Cosmic Egg," as the old occultists poetically expressed the idea.

The Rosicrucian concept of the World Soul—the First Manifestation—corresponds to similar conceptions found, in various forms, in most of the ancient occult teachings of the several great esoteric schools of philosophy. In some philosophies it is known as the "Anima Mundi," or Life of the World, Soul of the World, or World Spirit. In others it is known as the Logos, or Word. In others, as the Demiurge. The spirit of the concept is this: that from the unconditioned essence of Infinite Unmanifestation there arose an Elemental and Universal Soul, clothed in the garments of the most tenuous, elemental form of Matter, which contained within itself the potency

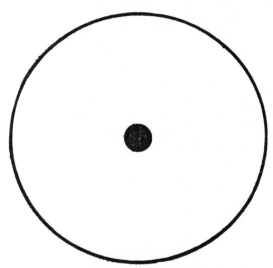

Figure 4. Symbol of the New-Born World Soul ("The Germ within the Egg")

and latent possibility of all the future universes of the new Cosmic Circle, or Cosmic Day. This World Soul is spoken of in the Second Aphorism as "The Germ within the Cosmic Egg," inasmuch as it is regarded as the tiny germ within the egg which gradually increases in size and complexity, and takes upon itself Form and Activity.

The symbol of the Cosmic Egg, of which the World Soul is the Animating Germ, is a very old one, and one widely spread in usage in the ancient world. As a prominent occultist has said: "Whence this universal symbol? The Egg was incorporated as a sacred sign in the cosmogony of every people on the earth, and was revered both on account of its form and its inner mystery. From the earliest mental conceptions of man, it was known as that which represented most successfully the Origin and Secret of Being. The gradual development of the imperceptible Germ within the closed shell; the inward working, without any apparent outward interference of force, which from a latent nothing produced an active something, needing nought save heat; and which, having gradually evolved into a concrete, living creature, broke its shell, appearing to the outward senses of all a self-generated, and self-created being—must have been a standing miracle from the beginning.

"The secret teaching explains the reason for this reference by the symbollism of the prehistoric races. The 'First Cause' had no name in the beginnings. Later, it was pictured in the fancy of the thinkers as an ever invisible Bird that dropped an Egg into Chaos, which Egg became the Universe. Hence, Brahm was called 'Kalahansa,' the Swan of Eternity which laid at the beginning of each Mahamanvantara a 'Golden Egg.' It typifies the great Circle, or O, itself a symbol for the universe and its spherical bodies. * * * The first manifestation of the Kosmos in the form of an egg was the most widely diffused belief of antiquity. It was a symbol adopted among the Greeks, the Syrians, Persians, and Egyptians. In the Egyptian Ritual, Seb, the god of Time and of the Earth, is spoken of as having laid an egg, or the Universe. Ra is shown like Brahma gestating

in the Egg of the Universe. With the Greeks the
Orphic Egg was a part of the Dionysiac and other
mysteries, during which the Mundane Egg was con-
secrated and its significance explained. The Chris-
tians—especially the Greek and Latin Churches—
have fully adopted this symbol, and see in it a com-
memoration of life eternal, or salvation and resur-
rection. This is found in and corroborated by the
custom of 'Easter Eggs.' From the 'Egg' of the
pagan Druids, to the red Easter Egg of the Slav, a
cycle has passed. And, yet, whether in civilized
Europe, or among the abject savages of Central
America, we find the same archaic, primitive
thought; if we only search for it and do not dis-
figure—in the haughtiness of our fancied mental
and physical superiority—the original idea of the
symbol.''

The concept of the World Soul, in some form of
interpretation and under some one of many names,
may be said to be practically universal. Among
many of the ancient schools of philosophy it was
taught that there was an Anima Mundi, or World
Soul, of which all the individual souls were but apparently separated (though not actually separated)
units. The conviction that Life was One is expressed through nearly all of the best of ancient
philosophies; and, in fact, in subtly disguised forms,
may be said to rest at the base of the best of modern
philosophies.

In the philosophical concept of the Logos, we find
another, and more advanced, form of this same
fundamental concept. The term, Logos, first became
prominent in the philosophy of Heraclitus of Ephe-
sus, where it appears as the Law of Nature, objective
in the world, giving order .and regularity to the

movement of things. The Logos formed an important part of the Stoic System of Philosophy. The Active Principle, abiding in the world, they called the Logos, the term being likewise applied to the Universal Productive Cause. An authority on the history of philosophy has said of the concept of the Logos: "The Logos, a being intermediate between ⌐⌐⌐ and the World, is diffused through the world ⌐⌐⌐ ⌐nses. The Logos does not exist from ⌐⌐ ⌐ke God, and yet its genesis is not like our ⌐wn and that of all other created beings. It is the First-Begotten of God, and is for us imperfect beings almost as a God. Through the agency of the Logos, God created the World."

In the philosophical concept of the Demiurge, we find another form of the same fundamental concept. The Demiurge was the name given by the Platonian philosophers to an exalted and mysterious agent by whom God was supposed to have created the universe. He was akin to the Nature-God of the Pantheists, and to the "Living Nature" of other schools of philosophy. The Demiurge was the Life of the World, or Universal Life, of which all the innumerable lives of finite creatures are but sparks in the flame or drops of water in the ocean. And, yet, in its true sense, the concept of the Demiurge was not identified with that of God, but was rather a concept of the First Great Manifestation of God, by means of which He creates and sustains the World.

The idea of a Universal Will, a primal manifestation of God, existing at the Heart of Nature, and operating to build up and sustain the Universe, is found in many modern philosophies. Cudsworth, the English philosopher has sought to indicate this conception in his idea of "Plastic Nature," of which he says: "It seems not so agreeable that Nature, as a distinct thing from the Deity, should be quite superseded or made to signifying nothing, God Himself doing all things immediately and miraculously; from whence it would follow also that they are all done either forcibly and violently, or else artificially only, and none of them by any inward principle of their own. This opinion is further confuted by that slow and gradual process that in the generation of things, which would seem to be but a vain and idle pomp or a trifling formality if the moving power were omnipotent; as also by those errors and bungles which are committed where the matter is inept and contumacious; which argue that the moving power be not irresistible, and that Nature is such a thing as is not altogether incapable (as well as human art) of being sometimes frustrated and disappointed by the indisposition of matter. Whereas an omnipotent moving power, as it could dispatch its work in a moment, so would it always do it infallibly and irresistibly, no ineptitude and stubborness of matter being ever able to hinder such a one, or make him bungle or fumble in anything.

"Therefore, since neither all things are produced fortuitously, or by the unguided mechanism of matter, nor God himself may be reasonably thought to do all things immediately and miraculously, it may well be concluded that there is a Plastic Nature under him, which, as an inferior and subordinate instrument, doth drudgingly execute that part of his providence which consists in the regular and orderly motion of matter; yet so as there is also besides this a higher providence to be acknowledged, which, presiding over it, doth often supply the defects of it, and sometimes overrules it, forasmuch as the Plastic

Nature cannot act electively nor with discretion:"

Other schools of philosophy, notably that founded by Schopenhauer, have postulated the presence of a Universal Spirit (whose chief attribute is Desire-Will) from whom the universe of creatures has proceeded. This Universal Spirit is held to be filled with a longing, craving, seeking, striving desire to express itself in phenomenal existence. Schopenhauer calls it "The Will to Live." It is described as **instinctive** rather than intellectual, and as creating intellect with which to better serve its purposes of self-expression. Other philosophers have proceeded along the main lines of the concept of Schopenhauer, with various modifications. The same idea is expressed by some of the old Buddhistic philosophers, the very term "The Will-to-Live" being used to express the essential nature of the Universal Spirit. But, it must be noted, in such philosophies the Universal Spirit is considered rather as the Eternal Parent than as its First Manifestation. In the same way a certain school of thinkers postulate the existence of a "Living Nature," which expresses itself in innumerable living creatures and things—all Things in the universe being held to possess Life in some form and degree, as, indeed, the Rosicrucian creatures also hold.

But it must be always noted that in the Secret Doctrine of the Rosicrucians the World Soul is not regarded as the Infinite Reality, but merely as the First Manifestation thereof, from which all subsequent manifestations proceed and into which they are finally resolved. The World Soul is not Eternal, but, on the contrary, appears and disappears according to the rhythm of the Cosmic Nights and Days.

The Second Aphorism states: **"The Flame is re-**

kindled." The Dark Light once more bursts into Flame throughout the form of the World Soul, and the new Universe begins.

It also states: **"Time begins."** This is seen to be true because Change has begun, and Change is the essence of Time, and Time the measure of Change.

Again: **"A Thing exists."** This because the World Soul is truly a Thing, with all the characteristics of Thingness. It can be defined and described in positive terms; it can be thought of logically and in terms of intellect, though perhaps not capable of being pictured in the imagination.

Again: **"Action begins."** This because from the very inception of the Germ in the Cosmic Egg there is the manifestation of Activity, Motion, and Change. The World Soul is in constant and uninterrupted activity from the moment of its faintest dawn until the moment of its expiring quiver.

Again: **"The Pairs of Opposites spring into being.** As all Thingness is accompanied by the presence of the Pairs of Opposites—the contrasting sets of qualities, it follows that from the first faint breath of the World Spirit differentiation begins, and the polarity of qualities exhibit themselves.

Again: **"The World Soul is born, and awakens into manifestation."** The World Soul awakens into active manifestation from the very moment of its birth. Finding within itself the impelling urge of the Will-to-Live and of Expression, it proceeds at once, along the lines of elementary Instinct to prepare for manifestation of higher and more complex forms of life and action.

Again: **"The first rays of the new Cosmic Day break over the horizon."** With the coming of the World Soul the new Cosmic Day is indeed begun, and proceeds without interruption until the shades of the Cosmic Night once more overtake it in cyclic sequence.

The Rosicrucian Teaching is that the World Soul is not a soul lacking a body, but that, on the contrary, it is clothed in the garments of the most tenuous and ethereal substance—a substance as much finer and more ethereal than the Ether of Space, of the material scientists, as the latter is much finer and more ethereal than the hardest steel or granite. From this ethereal substance the World Soul weaves bodies for its manifestations, even the densest forms of matter—and even the tenuous bodily form of the highest forms of life, far removed from our comparatively gross earth-plane.

The Rosicrucians further hold that it is not correct to think of the World Soul as having been created ''out of nothing'' by the Eternal Parent, and still less so think of it having been created from the substantial essence of the Eternal Parent by division, separation, or partition (such ideas being held to be logically impossible and fallacious). On the contrary, it is held that the World Soul exists as an IDEA of the Eternal Parent—just as, in a day dream, or a reverie, or a full dream, we may picture a Thing as in being. Or in other terms, even the World Soul exists merely as a PICTURE in the Infinite Imagination of the Eternal Parent, and at the last is but a SHADOW of Reality, and not Reality itself.

The World Soul, at the Dawn of the Cosmic Day, may be said to be like a dreamer freshly awakened from a deep sleep, and striving to regain consciousness of himself. It does not know what it is, nor does it know that it is but an Idea of the Eternal Parent. If it could express its thought in words it would say that it has always been, but had been asleep before that moment. It feels within itself the urge toward expression and manifestation, along unconscious and instinctive lines—this urge being a part of its nature and character and implanted into it by the content of the Idea of the Eternal Parent which brought it into being. Like the newborn babe, it struggles for breath and begins to move its limbs. And as it struggles and moves, there comes to it a response from all of its nature, and its active life begins. And here we leave the World Soul, for the moment, struggling for breath and striving to move its limbs (figuratively speaking, of course). Its future is related in the succeeding Aphorisms.

We are God's dream. — to awake, we are with God/as God. So stay in human existence — we stay separate in this dream. Ah Ha!

PART IV

THE UNIVERSAL ANDROGYNE

In the Secret Doctrine of the Rosicrucians, we find the following Third Aphorism:

The Third Aphorism

III. The One became Two. The Neuter became Bi-Sexual. Male and Female—the Two in One—evolved from the Neuter. And the work of Generation began.

In this Third Aphorism of Creation the Rosicrucian is directed to apply his attention to the conception of the World Soul—the First Manifestation of the Eternal Parent—as a Bi-sexual Universal Being. This Bi-Sexual Universal Being, combining within itself the elements and principles of both Masculinity and Femininity, is known in the Rosicrucian Teachings as "The Universal Hermaphrodite," and "The Universal Androgyne."

The term "Hermaphrodite" is defined as: "An individual which has the attributes of both Male and Female." The term is derived by joining together the two names, viz., Hermes and Aphrodite. The term came into ancient use through the legend of Hermaphroditus, son of Hermes and Aphrodite, who, while bathing, became joined in one body with the nymph Salmacis. The term "Androgyne" is defined as: "An individual possessing the attributes of both Male and Female; a Hermaphrodite." The term is derived from the combination of two Greek words, viz., "Andros," meaning "a man," and "Gyne," meaning "a woman."

The conception of the Bi-Sexuality in the Universal Manifestation, or Universal Being, is one met with on all sides in the ancient esoteric and occult philosophies in all lands. In ancient Greece, in

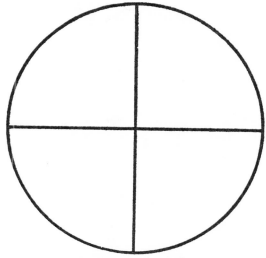

Figure 5. Symbol of the Universal Androgyne

Ancient India, and in Ancient Atlantis, Persia, and Chaldea the doctrine formed an important part of the Inner Teachings. In its highest forms, this teaching lay at the very heart of the Ancient Mysteries, and resulted in the very highest and noblest conception of the dignity and worthiness of Sex. But prostituted by the vulgar popular mind, encouraged by a debased priesthood, the same teachings were inverted and made to serve as the basis of the various degenerate phase of Phallic Worship, the traces of which are found on every page of ancient philosophical or religious history. The Rosicrucians have never countenanced even the slight descent into Phallicism, but, on the contrary have kept alive the Flame of the True Teaching, and have used its particular symbol as the distinctive symbolic name and emblem of the Order.

Figure 6. Symbol of the Phallic Cross.

In order to understand the symbology of the Universal Androgyne, it is necessary to first become familiar with the two ancient symbols of Sex. In all the ancient philosophies and religions, we find that the "Cross" (+) is the symbol of the Male; and the "Circle" (O) the symbol of the Female. In representing the Bisexual, the Hermaphrodite, the Androgyne, the two symbols, i. e. the Cross and the Circle are combined in one of several ways. The original way was that of placing the Cross within the circumference of the Circle; but later usage preferred the various forms of the so-called "Phallic Cross," which consists of the Circle, or Oval, sustaining the Cross which depends downward from it. (See illustrations.) Sometimes the Cross is represented as the letter "T", and the Circle as the letter "O".

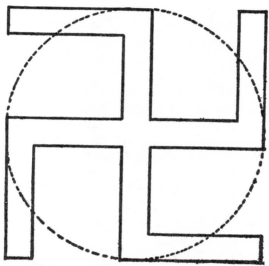

Figure 7. Symbol of the Swastica.

The well-known esoteric symbol, the "Swastica" (see illustration) consists of a modified Cross, conceived as a "whirling wheel" (something like the familiar spinning "pin wheel" of the boys' fireworks.) The whirling Cross of the Swastica, when seen in rapid motion, presents the appearance of a Circle enclosing a Cross.

This symbol of the "Circle enclosing the Cross" is one particularly sacred to the Rosicrucians, since to them it represents the Universal Activity and Uni-

versal Creation, symbolizing the Great Mystery of
Occult Generation on all planes of Life. In the fanciful symbology of the ancient Rosicrucian Brotherhoods, the Circle was transformed into the **Rose**,
and the Cross sometimes transformed into the Sword
with its Cross-like handle. The sign, then, of the
Cross (or Sword) combined with the Circle (or
Rose), symbolized the Mystic Union of the Rose and
the Cross, from whence arose the name of the Order,
i. e. Rosi-Crucian, meaning "Rose-Cross."

The Third Aphorism states: "**The One became
Two. The Neuter became Bi-Sexual. Male and
Female—the Two in One—evolved from the Neuter.
And the Work of Creation began.**"

In this Aphorism there is given the "hint" at the
very important teaching of the Rosicrucians concerning the Universal Sex Principles in Nature—the
presence and activity of the Sexual Pairs of Opposites, Male and Female, which constitute the Secret
of Creation. According to the Secret Doctrine of
the Rosicrucians, there are present in All-Creation
the activities of a Male Principle and a Female
Principle, both Universal in Nature, Character and
Extent—both Opposing Aspects of the World Soul
—which act and react, one upon the other, and thus
produce all Creative Activity and the "Cosmic Becoming" or Universal Activity and Change. And
the teachings also are that these Two Sex Principles
operate and manifest upon every plane of Life, from
the Sub-Mineral, on to the Mineral, on to the Plant,
on to the Animal, on to the Human, or to the Super-
Human, on to the Angelic or God-like. And, likewise,
that in every Thing in Creation there is present and
manifest the activity of Sex.

The above statement of the Universality of Sex

may seem somewhat surprising to the person who has not acquainted himself, or herself, with the Ancient Wisdom of the Esoteric Schools; or who is not familiar with the daring conceptions of advanced modern science. But to that one who has mastered the ancient wisdom-teachings, and who has likewise become acquainted with the best of modern advanced scientific thought, there will seem nothing strange about these statements. The ancient teachings taught positively that there was present and active Sex in all Manifestated Creation; and Modern Science is beginning to teach that the evidence of the presence of Sex in every Thing is conclusive.

The ancient teachings, which were later embodied in the early Rosicrucian teachings, held that in order that there might be Becoming, Change, or Creation, there must be Re-action following Action—the play of one force on another. And the best teachings of the ancients were that these two opposing forces in Nature were Masculine, and Feminine, respectively —dual aspects of the Universal Being. And Modern Science is fast coming to recognize and teach the same great truth.

The best teachings of modern science is that there is a stimulating or fertilizing activity in nature which acts upon a generative force, the latter reacting upon the former. And, at the other end of the material scale, we find the teaching that the atom (once supposed to be the ultimate form of matter) is now discovered to be composed of a multitude of electrons, corpuscles, or ions (different names for the same thing) revolving around each other at a tremendous rate of motion. It was formerly supposed that the electrons simply revolved one around another, and that all were alike in character and nature; but the later discoveries show that the formation of the atom is due rather to the action of numerous circling positive (or "male") electrons around a central negative (or "female") electron, the positive (or "male") electrons seemingly exerting a peculiar effect upon the negative (or "female") electron, causing her to put forth certain energies which result in the "generation" of the atomic structure.

This is in perfect accordance with the old Rosicrucian doctrine that the "positive" pole of magnetism and electricity (for both were well known to the ancient alchemists) was "masculine," and that the "negative" pole of the same was "feminine." But, unfortunately, the terms "positive" and "negative," respectively are used with the wrong implication and much confusion results therefrom. For instance, the term "positive" is used to indicate strength and reality, as opposed to weaknesses and unreality of the "negative." But the real facts of physical science show us the falsity of such an interpretation of these terms. The so-called "negative" pole of the battery is really the pole of generation or the production of new forms and energies— the best authorities now prefer to use the term "the cathode pole" in place of "the negative;" the word "cathode" being derived from the Greek word meaning "descent; the path of generation," etc. From the "cathode" pole of the battery emerge the great swarms of electrons, ions, or corpuscles; and from the same pole also emerge the wonderful "rays" which have played such an important part in modern physics. The "cathode" pole of the battery is the Mother of all that strange brood of new forms of matter which have appeared to confute the old materialistic theories, and to destroy the old conceptions of science. The "cathode" pole should, in reality and truth, be called the "female" pole; and the "positive" the "male," for such terms truly represent their true respective offices.

Modern science also teaches that the electrons which are "composed of negative (female) electricity," frequently becomes detached from its male companion corpuscles, and starts on an independent career. It seeks a union with a masculine corpuscle, and gaining it a new set of creative activity is begun. When the female corpuscle unites with the new masculine one a strange phenomenon occurs; the corpuscles began vibrating and circling around each other, and the result is the birth of a new atom in which is combined the masculine and feminine energies in some particular proportion. The atom, thus formed, does not manifest the properties of free electricity but manifests an entirely new set of properties. The process of detachment of the feminine electrons is called "ionization;" and arising from such detachments and the formation of new unions result the varied phenomena of heat, light, electricity, magnetism, etc.

In the same way, the varied phenomena of "chemical attraction" and "chemical affinity" arise from the manifestation of Sex on the atomic plane, though science has not as yet perceived this to be the truth. Science teaches that there are "marriages, divorces, and re-marriages" among the atoms, but it hesitates to go further and assert that this is a part of the universal Sex manifestation—but this announcement must come in time for the evidence is overwhelmingly convincing. The explosive properties of certain substances really result from a "divorce" of the atomic and molecular parties—the detachment of the male and female particles under the influence of a stronger attraction; and the formation of the different substances result from the attractive unions of certain male and female elements of matter. Alchemy has always known this to be a fact; it remains for modern science to corroborate and reaffirm the "vagaries" of the old alchemists regarding this important fact of nature.

It has always been admitted by science that there was Sex manifest in plant-life as well as by animal-life, but the mineral-life was not given the benefit of the manifestation of the universal principle of Sex. But recent discoveries have forced upon scientists the fact that in the crystallization of minerals there is an unmistakable evidence of the presence and activity of Sex, and in the near future it will be found that all the other changes in minerals are the result of Sex-attraction or repulsion. And, as we shall see in a subsequent chapter of this book, there is present the activity of Sex on the mental planes of life.

In short, on each and every plane of Life, physical, mental, or spiritual there is found present and active the Universal Principle of Sex, in some of its phases and forms. Sex cannot be escaped in Nature—the Universe is Bi-Sexual, and all Creation, on every plane, is caused by Sex and Sex only. A full understanding of this important fact would revolutionize the conceptions of modern science, and render practicable many important ideas which now exist merely as dreams in the minds of the advanced scientists. To those who cannot see this plainly, we would say: It is admitted that all physical and mental phenomena depend for activity upon the Law of

Attraction. When it is discovered that the law of Attraction proceeds along the lines of Sex, and Sex alone, then it is seen that all activity is Sex-Activity.

Had the World-Soul remained Neuter, there would have been no Universal Manifestation or Creation. It was necessary that the Principle of Sex should appear, in order that Creation should begin. It is only by the constant and continuous action and reaction of the Two Sex Principles in Nature that Creation, Process, Becoming, and Change is possible —and as all Things are but the products of Change, Process, Becoming, and Creation, it follows that without Sex there would have been to Things in the Universe—and in that even the World Soul would have abided apart, alone, and single until the end of its days. With the introduction of Sex came the beginning of Generation and Creation, under which the One became the Many and Sameness became Variety and Diversity. The ancient teachings furnish the only logical explanation of Creation. The One becomes the Two, and from the Two proceed the Many.

PART V

THE ONE AND THE MANY

In the Secret Doctrine of the Rosicrucians, we find the following Fourth Aphorism:

The Fourth Aphorism

IV. The One becomes Many. The Unity becomes Diversity. The Identical becomes Variety. Yet the Many remains One; the Diversity remains Unity; and the Variety remains Identical.

In this Fourth Aphorism of Creation, the Rosicrucian is directed to apply his attention to the concept of the World Soul—the First Manifestation of the Eternal Parent—as a One Manifesting as Many; a Unity manifesting as Diversity; an Identical manifesting as Variety: yet, nothwithstanding such manifestations, remaining ever One, Unity, and Identical.

This concept of the World Soul, so manifesting itself in Manifoldness, Diversity, and Variety, yet ever remaining One, Unity, and Identical, is represented by the Rosicrucians by the symbol of a small circle within a larger circle, the smaller circles being filled with tiny points or centres of manifestation. The outer circle is, of course, the Infinite Unmanifest; the smaller circle, of course, being the World Soul; and the small dots, or points, being the individualized centres of life, being, and activity manifested by the World Soul.

That all beings are, in truth, but expressions of

the One Being—centres of consciousness, form, and activity within itself,—is a fundamental tenet of all occult and esoteric teaching. That all Being is One; all Life, One; all Form, One; all Consciousness, One, is known to all true disciples of the occult and esoteric teachings of the past and present, occidental and oriental, philosophical and theological. Hidden

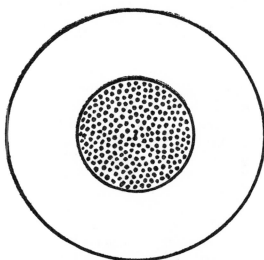

Figure 8. Symbol of the Many in the One

behind and under the orthodox, exoteric teachings, there is always to be found this insistence upon Essential Oneness on the part of the Inner Teachings of all schools.

That there is but One Life, and not Many Lives, is a fundamental article of all occult and esoteric faith. The One Life, moreover, is not to be thought of as dividing and splitting itself up into bits, parts, and particles, in order to accomplish the process of Creation, and the Manifestation of the World. Instead, it is to be thought of as merely **reflecting** itself in the many individual mirrors of expression, just as the sun reflects itself as One in the millions of falling raindrops, or in a million tiny jars filled with water. There are millions of reflections of the One, but only the one One in reality. Or, using another figure of speech, the One may be thought of as an Infinite Ocean of Being, in which there are millions of tiny bubbles, each apparently apart and separate, but all of which are in reality, but centres of activity and expression in the One Great Ocean.

Separateness is, to quote a writer, "but the working fiction of Creation." All the apparently separated Things are contained within the circle of the World Soul—and the latter is contained within the circle of the Infinite Unmanifest.

Not only is this esoteric conception of the Many in One, and the One in Many, a fundamental conception of the ancient esoteric and occult teachings, but the same truth in another form is presented by advanced modern science in its conception of the Universal Substance. Science postulates the existence of a Universal Substance, known under many names, from which all Things proceed. It matters not whether this Universal Substance be called "Primordial Substance," or "Infinite and Eternal Energy," or "The Universal Ether," the fact remains that science postulates its existence as a fundamental, substantial Something, of and in which all forms and phases of phenomenal existence are but manifestations. In the same way, those schools of transcendental philosophy which postulate the existence of a Universal Mind teach that all forms and phases of phenomenal existence are but Thought Forms in the Universal Mind. And the old Brahmanical teachings likewise hold that the Many exist but as incidents of the "dream" or "meditation" of the Lord High Brahma.

In all forms, phases, and schools of philosophy we find this insistence upon the presence and existence of a One Something of which all else are but manifestations. In fact, as the wisest philosophers have informed us, the whole purpose of philosophy is to discover the One Unconditioned Ground of all that exists Conditionally. All philosophy worthy of the name is Monistic in essence. A leading authority on the history of philosophy informs us the: "Monism is, in strictness, a name applicable to any system of thought which sees in the universe the manifestation or working of a single principle. Such a unity may be at once the tacit presupposition and the goal of all philosophic effect, and in so far as a philosophy fails to harmonize the apparently independent and even conflicting facts of experience, as aspects or elements within a larger whole, it must be held to fall short of the necessary ideal of thought. Dualism, in an ultimate metaphysical reference, is a confession of the failure of philosophy to achieve its proper task; and this is a justification of those who consistently use the word as a term of reproach."

And, now, let us take a brief passing glance at the Rosicrucian teachings concerning the manner in which the One proceeded to become the Many—the Unity to become Diversity—the Identical to become Variety—and yet remain the One, Unity, Identity of the World Soul, unaffected and unchanged by its plunge into Manifestation. Evolution we see on all sides around us, but all Evolution must be preceded by Involution, as all occultists and scientists know full well.

Modern Science, in pursuing its discoveries along the lines of Evolution, has almost entirely ignored the twin-activity of Manifestation, which is known as Involution. Not so the ancient occultists, however, for they knew full well the truth so forcibly expressed in the words of a modern "plain speaking" philosopher who said: "You can never get out of a thing anything which is not already involved in it." And to the ancient student of the esoteric teachings any idea of Evolution which did not begin with the teachings concerning Involution was like the play of Hamlet with Hamlet left out. There is an ancient saying which runs: "That which is evolved must previously have been involved;" and in this simple statement is condensed a volume of important occult lore.

The term "Involve" means "to wrap up; to cover; to hide; etc." The term "Evolve" means "to unwrap; to unfold; to un-roll; etc." With these meanings in mind, the student sees at once that before a thing can be "unwrapped, un-folded, un-rolled," it must have first been wrapped-up, folded-up, rolled-up. We must not lose sight of the meaning attached to the simple terms, no matter how many high-sounding terms are substituted for these. The same thing remains the same thing, no matter how many new names are attached to it.

The esoteric teachings, as has been said, clearly and positively state that before there began the wonderful process of Evolution from simple to more complex forms of manifestation—from lower to higher —there must first have been an "involution" or infolding of the World Soul into the simple, gross, elemental forms of matter. The vibrations must have been first lowered, before they can have been increased.

Plunging at once, with terrific speed and force, into the abyss of Manifestation, the World Soul created for itself material garments of the densest and grossest elemental matter. This extreme form of elemental matter is not known to us today, for it has been discarded in the course of evolution on this particular planet. It, however, still exists on other planets of our solar system. This form, or forms, of elemental matter is below the scale of the minerals, and is as much lower than the grossest mineral known to science as that mineral is lower than the highest plant. In texture, structure, and density the extreme form of elemental matter is as much grosser than the lowest form of mineral known to us, as the latter is grosser than the highest form of ethereal vapor or radiant matter known to modern science. It is useless to try to describe this form of matter, for the ordinary mind cannot grasp it in the absence of concrete illustration.

When the lowest point in the scale of Involution was reached, then the Law of Rhythm asserted itself, and the upward climb began—the first movement of Evolution began to manifest itself. And, at this precise point, there was begun the manifestation of what may be termed "individualization," or the forming of centres of activity and consciousness. The World Soul descended into the depth of Involution enmasse, and then began to emerge from those depths by an apparent "splitting up" process, in which the active new-born centres of activity began to assert themselves and to move upward toward self-expression. The simpler centres which occultists know to be the centers of activity in the electrons of matter began to form molecules. There was of course manifested the presence of mind within this gross matter—but only the faint glimmerings were manifested, for the gross enveloping sheaths of matter almost smothered the mental principles involved within them.

The Process of Evolution once begun, it proceeded rapidly. Higher and higher in the scale of manifestation rose the Things—in spiralic process, each spiral rising above the one beneath it, and yet each proceeding apparently in a circle, as do all proceeding things. In due time the first signs of the mineral kingdom began to show themselves, building upon the basis of the sub-mineral forms of matter. In the mineral kingdom began to manifest higher forms of life and mind—for, as the occultists know well, the minerals possess both life and mind in a certain degree. And then later appeared the first signs of plant life—forms but slightly above those of certain crystals.

When the temperature of the earth was at a point at which life is commonly believed to be impossible, there were present certain strange forms of life, which may be described as half mineral—half plant. These crystals reproduced themselves by a splitting up process, and grew from the inside as do plants. These life forms were composed of the same materials as the crystals from which they evolved—but they possessed a greater degree of life and mind, and while from one point of view they may be said to have been minerals, yet from another they may truly be said to have been plants. These strange creatures have disappeared as have all other ''intermediate forms'' which have played the parts of bridges in the evolutionary process. But they have left their traces in the material bodies of both plants and animals. For it must be remembered that even the bodies of the highest forms of plant or animal life are composed of certain chemical elements which were derived from the mineral kingdom, as for instance, oxygen, hydrogen, carbon, nitrogen, sulphur, phosphorus, etc.

The first forms of real plant life are described by the old teachers as having been a now-extinct lowly form of plant-life scarcely more than a crystal in appearance, and yet manifesting the characteristics of plant life. Then appeared the ancestors of what are now known as the "chlomacea" which are a strange group of lowly creatures, comprising the characteristics of both plant and mineral life, and being found even today in the deposits upon damp rocks, the bark of trees, etc. From this and simpler creatures evolved the ancestors of what are now known as the "angiospores," or lowest forms of plant-life; and later, the ancestors of the "gymnospores," which are probably the lowest forms of animal-life known to science today.

The Process of Evolution is caused by the constant striving of the Life and Mind within the sheaths of matter—the striving to express more and still more of themselves, and to mould and use the sheaths of matter in the work of self-expression. Protoplasm, the physical basis of plant and animal life, was evolved in this way. Then came the single-celled creature which dwelt in the slime of the ancient ocean beds. Then forms of life composed of colonies of cells appeared. Then more complex forms of cell-combination, and so on, and on, until the highest forms of life known to us today were evolved.

Finally, primitive man was evolved. Then man

began to improve in mind and feeling. And he is still making progress along these lines. But man (of today) is merely a high stage of the evolutionary process, and he, in turn, will be succeeded by the Super-Men of the future, and these in turn by the god-like angelic creatures, the like of whom are in existence on other and high spheres even this day.

But always remember that in all the millions of types of living forms, and the millions upon millions upon millions of individuals ensouling these forms, there is no real separateness. All life is One—and all Life but the Life of the World Soul. Therefore, in the symbol of the Rosicrucians—the countless points within the smaller circle, which in turn is enclosed within the larger circle—we have the picture of the Eternal Parent and its First Manifestation, the World Soul, the latter manifesting in the countless life-forms of the World of Manifestation. And, the work of Evolution is still underway, and higher and higher forms of expression will proceed from within the Involved Being of the World Soul which is ever striving and struggling to manifest itself in self-expression.

PART VI

THE UNIVERSAL FLAME OF LIFE

In the Secret Doctrine of the Rosicrucians, we find the following Fifth Aphorism:

The Fifth Aphorism

V. The One is the Flame of Life. The Many are the Sparks in the Flame. The Flame once lighted kindles everything within its sphere. The Fire is in everything and everywhere; there is nothing dark or cold within its sphere.

In this Fifth Aphorism of Creation, the Rosicrucian is directed to apply his attention to the concept of the Universal Life—the Life of the World Soul, permeating everything everywhere within its sphere of existence. This concept of the World Soul as a Flaming Fire of Life, abiding in the entire Universe in all of its parts, is represented by the Rosicrucians by the symbol of a circle filled with flaming fire.

The symbol of Life has always been the Flaming Fire, in all occult teachings. The Eternal, Universal Fire, or Flame, which kindles ever all that presents itself to its influence, yet ever remains unchanged and undiminished in its Essence, has ever been the favorite symbol of the occultists for the Universal Life in Manifestation. When the term "Spirit" is used to indicate "Life," then the Flame or Fire has always been the symbol for Spirit.

And, indeed, the Flame is the most appropriate

symbol for Life that can be thought of. For the Flame while ever remaining the same, yet is never composed of the same particles or sparks for even two consecutive seconds. The Flame, itself, in its Essence, ever remains the same and unchanged, yet its Manifestation is always accompanied and correlated to the appearance and disappearance of in-

Figure 9. Symbol of the Universal Flame of Life

numerable tiny particles of material substance which it kindles into sparks, then destroys by the process of combustion, and then replaces by others of similar nature.

And so it is with the Universal Life. It ever persists unchanged and unaltered in its Essence, yet constantly manifesting itself through and in countless material forms which come and go and are in turn replaced by other forms. The form appears, is consumed, and perishes—yet the Flame abides and survives all change. Those who have plunged deep into the esoteric teachings are aware that there are many other very good reasons why the Flame or Fire is the best possible symbol for Life, but it is not thought expedient to go into these further reasons at this time and in this place.

It was formerly the teachings of science that the Universe was composed of two great classes of Things, as follows: (1) Living Things, and (2) Lifeless Things. In the first class were placed all human and animal life, at least during their term of vital existence; plants were afterward added, though somewhat grudgingly, by science. In the second class, all Things below the plane of animal or plant life were placed; it being taught that minerals, chemical elements, etc., were utterly lifeless. Any who ventured to question this accepted classification were deemed of unsound mind, and unworthy of serious consideration.

But the esoteric schools of thought, and the occultists, were always insistent upon the principle that there was nothing lifeless in the universe—that everything was instinct with life in some form, degree, or phase. And, lo! modern science has at last reached the point where it is practically looking Occultism squarely in the face, in full agreement upon this important point. The old idea of a half-lifeless universe is fast passing away, and men of advanced science are beginning to whisper to each other that "The Universe is Alive, as a Whole and in all of its parts." Surely this is a remarkable change in scientific opinion.

This changed conception of science is picturesquely expressed by Luther Burbank, the "wizard of plant life," as follows: "All my investigations have led me away from the idea of a dead material universe tossed about by various forces, to that of a universe which is absolutely all force, life, soul, thought, or whatever name we may choose to call it. Every atom, molecule, plant, animal, or planet, is only an aggregation of organized unit forces, held in place by stronger forces, thus holding them for a time latent, though teeming with inconceivable power. All life on our planet is, so to speak, just on the outer fringe of this infinite ocean of force. The universe is not half-dead, but all alive.''

Prof. Dolbear goes back even to the Ether of Space in his assumption of Omnipresent Life, when he says: ''The Ether has besides the function of energy and motion, other inherent qualities, out of which could emerge under proper circumstances, other phenomena, such as life, mind, or whatever may be in that substratum.'' Prof. Cope has intimated that ''the basis of Life lies back of the atoms and may be found in the Universal Ether.''

Saleeby, in his well-known work of Evolution, in which he carries to its logical conclusions the work of Herbert Spencer, says: ''Life is potential in matter; life-energy is not a thing unique and created at a particular time in the past. If evolution be true, living matter has been evolved by natural processes from matter which is, apparently, dead. But if life is potential in matter, it is a thousand times more evident that mind is potential in life. The evolutionist is impelled to believe that mind is potential in matter. (I adopt that form of words for the moment, but not without future criticism.) The microscopic cell, a minute speck of matter that is to become man, has in it the promise and germ of mind. May we not draw the inference that the elements of mind are present in those chemical elements—carbon, oxygen, hydrogen, nitrogen, sulphur, phosphorus, sodium, potassium, chlorine—that are found in the cell. Not only must we do so, but we must go further, since we know that each of these elements, and every other, is built up out of one invariable unit, the electron, and we must therefore assert that mind is potential in the unit of matter—the electron itself. It is to assert the sublime truth first perceived by Spinoza, that mind and matter are the warp and woof of what Goethe called 'the living garment of God.' Both are complementary expressions of the Unknowable Reality which underlies both.''

Flammarion has said: ''The universe is a dynamism. Life itself, from from the most rudimentary cell up to the most complicated organism, is a special kind of movement, a movement determined and organized by a directing force. Visible matter, which stands for us at the present moment for the universe, and which certain classic doctrines consider as the origin of all things—movement, life, thought—is only a word void of meaning. The universe is a great organism, controlled by a dynamism of the psychical order. Mind gleams through its every atom. There is mind in everything, not only in human and animal life, but in plants, in minerals, in space.'' [The student must always remember that where there is ''mind,'' there must be ''life;'' and where ''life,'' there must be ''mind.'' Hence the importance of these admissions of modern science.]

Haeckel in his ''Riddle of the Universe,'' sometimes called ''The Bible of Materialism,'' makes the following statement, remarkable coming from such a source: ''I cannot imagine the simplest chemical and physical process, without attributing the movements of the material particles to unconscious sensation." Again, he says: "The idea of chemical affinity consists in the fact that the various chemical elements perceive the qualitative differences in other elements—experience 'pleasure' or 'revulsion' at contact with them, and execute specific movements on this ground." He adds, at another point: "The sensations and responses in plant and animal life are connected by a long series of evolutionary stages with the simpler forms of sensation that we find in the inorganic elements, and that reveal themselves in chemical affinity." He quotes with approval the statement of Nageli that: "If the molecules possess something that is related, however distantly, to sensation, it must be uncomfortable to be able to follow their attractions and repulsions; uncomfortable when they are forced to do otherwise."

But not only is modern science giving approval to the oldest conceptions of the occultists concerning Universal Life in the manner mentioned above, i. e. by general statements; it is also quoting with approval the experiments and discoveries of leading scientists along the same line—experiments which go to prove the general statements above quoted. Let us consider a few of these experiments and discoveries in the laboratories of modern science.

Science has practically created counterparts of the diatoms or "living crystals"—created artificially, in the laboratories, creatures similar to these links between the mineral and the animal forms. The diatoms are tiny geometrical forms, composed of a tiny shell of siliceous material enclosing a minute drop of plasm, resembling glue. These creatures are visible through the microscope, and are so small that thousands of them might be gathered together on the head of a pin. They so closely resemble crystals that a very careful examination is required to distinguish them from true crystals; and yet they are alive, and perform all the functions of life.

Crystals, as you know, are born, grow, live, and may be killed by chemicals or electricity. Some investigators have discovered indications of elementary sex functions in certain crystals. A scientific writer has said: "Crystallization, as we are to learn now, is not a mere mechanical grouping of dead atoms—it is a birth." The crystal forms from the mother liquor, and its body is built up systematically, regularly, and according to a well-defined pattern, plan, or design—as true to the pattern as are the bodies of plants and animals. The certainty is present in the crystal creative life activity. And, not only does the crystal grow in this way, like a plant or an animal, but it also reproduces itself by separation and division, just as do the individuals of the lower forms of plant-life and animal-life. The distinguishing point between the growth and reproduction of crystal forms and that of the higher forms of life has, heretofore, been held to be as follows: the crystal takes its nourishment from the outside and builds up its bodily structure on its outer surface, while the lowly forms of plant-life and animal-life takes its nourishment from the outside but builds up its bodily structure from within. If the crystal had a soft-centre and took its nourishment in the way of the low form of plant-life or animal-life (building from within) it would be almost identical with the diatom; or if the diatom grew from the outside, and had a hard centre, it would be considered a true crystal; so, as you see there is very little real difference between them. And, now, lo! even this distinction is apparently to be wiped out by the discovery of artificial living crystals, evolved in the laboratory.

Careful scientific tests have determined that there is what is known as "the fatigue of elasticity" in metals, which is relieved by a rest or "vacation." This has also been found true of razors, the edges of which are restored by a little rest, thus corroborating the ancient "superstition" of users of razors. Tuning forks have been found to lose their power of vibration by over-use, a short rest restoring the same. Machinery in mills and factories have been found to be benefited by an occasional "day off." Metals have been discovered to be subject to disease and infection, and in some cases have been found to have been actually poisoned and afterward restored by antidotes. Window glass, especially the fine stained glass of cathedral windows, is found to be subject to an infectious disease, spreading from pane to pane, and resulting in the disintegration of the substance of the glass. Workmen's tools have been found to experience fatigue, and to be the better for an occasional holiday or longer vacation. Every observing machinist has observed certain idiosyncrasies in particular machines which need "humoring."

The most conclusive scientfic report upon this interesting subject, so far as known to the present writer, is that which recites the celebrated series of experiments conducted upon so-called "non-living matter, several years ago, and which are recorded in the book entitled "Response in the Living and Non-Living," by the scientists who conducted the experiments, Professor J. Chunder Bose, of the Calcutta University, who occupies a high position in the scientific world. Professor Bose's experiments have aroused the greatest interest in prominent scientific circles, and have aided greatly in corroborating the conclusions of other scientists who hold that "there is no such thing as dead matter."

Proceeding from the fundamental postulate that the best and only true test of the presence of life is the response of matter to external stimulus, Professor Bose has demonstrated that in many instances so-called inorganic matter, such as metals, minerals, etc., give a response to such stimulus which is similar, if not indeed identical, to the response of the matter composing the bodies of "living" animals, plants, and men. He devised certain very delicate apparatus for registering and measuring such responses, the same being traced as curves on a revolving cylinder. He employed that most delicate scientific instrument called the Galvanometer in these experiments. The Galvanometer will register the faintest irritation of nerve-matter, or living muscle; and the experiments proved that it would also register the variations of minerals, metals, etc., subjected to the stimulus of outside force; the curves or tracings being practically identical in either case.

Professor Bose reports that when he attached the Galvanometer to bars of various metals they gave a similar response when struck or twisted; the greater the degree of irritation caused in the metal the greater the degree of response. It should be noted that the living nerve or muscle reacts and registers in precisely the same way, and so far as the instrument indicated the response of muscle, nerve, metal, and mineral was identical. Just as the nerve or registered "fatigue" after frequently repeated stimulus, so did the metal or mineral so register. And, just as the nerve or muscle registered the renewal of vigor after a rest, so did the metal or mineral. To all intents and purposes the "living" and "non-living" matter gave the same response and evidence of "life." Moreover, the instrument showed something like "tetanus" in metals, caused by repeated shocks; recovery after the rest being also recorded. Moreover, several metals recorded fatigue from other causes; and in some cases the metals showed the effect of poisoning, recovery by the application of antidotes, and also the signs of excitement or intoxication from other forms of stimulus.

The experiments also showed that metals manifest a condition akin to sleep; that they can be killed; that they exhibit torpor and sluggishness; that they wake up, and can be roused into activity; that they may be stimulated, strengthened, weakened, drugged or intoxicated; that they suffer from extreme cold or heat; that they respond to the presence of certain drugs just as do living plant and animal. A piece of steel subjected to the effect of poison recorded on the delicate instrument a gradual fluttering and weakening, resulting in final death, just as does a portion of animal matter, or an organ of the body of an animal, or a piece of the living substance of a plant. When revived before it was too late, the response of the metal was gradual in the case of both muscle and metal. A most interesting fact is the statement of the experimentor that even the poisons which served to "kill" the metals showed a like susceptibility to the actions of other poisons, and were found to be, themselves, capable of being "killed" by poisons. In the case of these metal "killings," however, the molecular structure was apparently not affected, just as the similar structure in the animal tissue is not affected—in both cases there was apparently a causing of a "something within" to cease to function in the substance, a "something" which may as well be called a "soul" as any other term.

Other scientific laboratory experiments have revealed most interesting facts concerning the production of living things from "non-living matter." Dr. Charles Bastian, of London, England, has prepared and exhibited more than five thousand microphotographs showing the evolution of organic living forms from the inorganic "non-living" (so-called). He claims to have produced certain microscopic black spots from a previously perfectly clear liquor, which spots gradually enlarge and are transformed into certain forms of lowly bacteria. Professor Burke, of Cambridge, England, claims to have produced from sterilized bouillon, by the action of sterilized radium chloride, certain minute living bodies which manifest subsequent growth and reproduction by subdivision.

The ordinary student of chemistry and physics is familiar with what is called "metallic vegetation," notably in the case of the "lead tree," in which there is manifested the appearance of plant forms on the part of the acidulated solution of certain metallic substances. In the case of the "lead tree" an acidulated solution of acetate of lead is placed in a wide-necked bottle, from the cork of which bottle a piece of copper wire is suspended, at the end of which dangles a piece of zinc which hangs at the centre of the lead solution. When the bottle is corked the copper wire begins at once to be surrounded with a growth of metallic lead closely resembling a very fine moss, which moss gradually develops branches and limbs and finally foliage, in the end a miniature bush or tree being formed. Other metallic solutions produce similar phenomena. Saltpeter, subjected to the effect of polarized light, assumes forms closely resembling the orchid. Crystals of frost form on window panes the shapes of leaves, branches, foliage, blossoms, flowers, etc. Many metals tend to crystallize in the forms of vegetable growth; and this is particularly significant when it is remembered that crystals are beginning to be regarded as ''almost alive'' by modern science, as noted in a preceding paragraph of the present chapter.

The scientific magazines, a few years ago, contained references to an interesting experiment performed by a German scientist using certain metallic salts. The scientist subjected the salts to the action of a galvanic current, and was astounded to discover that around the negative or cathode (female) pole of the battery the particles of the metallic salt began to group themselves in the form of a tiny mushroom, with stem and umbrella-like top. These metallic mushrooms at first displayed a transparent appearance, but gradually developed color, and finally assumed a pale straw color on the stems, with a bright red color on the top of the umbrella and a faint rose tint on the under surface. But the most startling feature of the phenomenom was that the metallic mushroom had fine veins or tiny tubes running along the interior of the stems, through which the nourishment, or additional material for growth, was transported—the mushroom **being fed from the inside,** as in the case of the true fungus mushroom. It seemed that, to all intents and purposes, these metallic mushrooms were practically the connecting link between mineral and vegetable life.

As has been stated elsewhere in this chapter, modern science now stands on the threshold of the discovery (by actual laboratory proof) that there is no such thing as "lifeless" matter—and that Everything is Alive. This has been the contention of the occultists for thousands of years. As a writer has said, it would seem that as in the case of the great Tunnel of the Alps, the two bands of workers, each on its own side of the mountain, were fast approaching the place where only a thin partition separated them one from another; and that already they can faintly hear the sounds of each others' picks penetrating the thin dividing wall between the two camps. The occultist may now safely await the day when modern science will actually "prove for him the old teaching of the esoteric schools."

Moreover, science is coming very near to the place when it will perceive the truth of the old occult axiom that "All Power is Will-Power," and that the movements of electrons, atoms, molecules, and masses of matter are in response to an inward "feeling" resulting from the attraction or repulsion to or from other forms of matter, and the "will" action in response thereto, as Haeckel and Nageli (materialistic scientists though they may be called) have claimed for half a generation past. The contention of the Materialists that Life and Mind are but qualities of Matter, and are to be found in all forms of material objects, needs but to be **inverted** in order to show the Truth, long since uttered by the ancient occultists, namely that Matter is but the Outer Garment of **Soul** (Life-Mind), and that all material forms are ensouled by Life and Mind. The conception of the Materialists is but the Inverted Pyramid of Error, while the conception of the Occultists is the firmly placed, and soundly resting, true Pyramid of Truth—that Rock of Ages which can never be overturned, for it rests squarely and firmly on the Eternal Base of Being.

Remember, O student, the Rosicrucian aphorism that **"The Fire is in everything and everywhere: there is nothing dark or cold within its sphere."**

PART VII

THE PLANES OF CONSCIOUSNESS

In the Secret Doctrine of the Rosicrucians, we find the following Sixth Aphorism:

The Sixth Aphorism

VI. As Life is the Essence of Spirit, so is Consciousness the Essence of Life. Spirit is One, yet it manifests in many forms of Life. Life is One, yet it manifests in many forms of Consciousness. While the forms of manifested Consciousness are innumerable, yet the wise know Consciousness to manifest on Seven Planes: and these Planes of Consciousness are known to the wise as (1) The Plane of the Elements; (2) The Plane of the Minerals; (3) The Plane of the Plants; (4) The Plane of the Animals; (5) The Plane of the Human; (6) The Plane of the Demi-Gods; (7) The Plane of the Gods.

In this Sixth Aphorism of Creation, the Rosicrucian is directed to apply his attention to the concept of Life-Consciousness manifesting on its seven planes. This concept is represented by the Rosicrucians by means of the symbol of a linked chain of seven circles, each link penetrating the one on either side of it.

The Sixth Aphorism wisely states that "Life is the Essence of Spirit." No matter what else Spirit may be, or may not be, it cannot be denied that Spirit must possess the attribute of Life, in order to be Spirit. Likewise, the Aphorism states: "Consciousness is the Essence of Life," which is also self-evident; for no matter what else Life may be, or may not be, it cannot be denied that Life must possess the attribute of Life.

A modern writer has well said that "Mind is the Livingness of Life," and, of course, Mind is naught

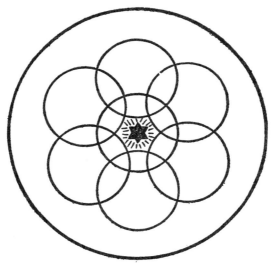

Figure 10. Symbol of the Seven Planes of Consciousness

but a term employed to indicate "states of consciousness." Even the average person implicitly testifies to the fact of the necessary presence of Consciousness in Life by his distinctions between the various forms of living things. The higher the manifestation of Consciousness in a living thing, the higher the degree of "Life" he attributes to it; and when the indications of Consciousness are lacking, he pronounces the thing "lifeless." The proof of conscious activity among mineral forms at once leads to the thought that "then minerals must be alive." Consciousness, in its essence, manifests as "the attribute of receiving impressions from outside stimuli, and the power to respond thereto;" and the student will at once recognize this attribute as the fundamental test of living substance.

Just as the Rosicrucians hold as a fundamental doctrine the teaching that "Everything is Alive" (see preceding chapter), so do they hold as equally fundamental the teaching that "Everything is Conscious." But, here is where half-knowledge is apt to fall into a trap, and to attribute to the Rosicrucian beliefs quite foreign to them. For in the Rosicrucian teachings (and in the most advanced modern psychology, as well) the term "consciousness" is not restricted to those phases of consciousness most familiar to us, but, rather, to all forms of "awareness," whether higher or lower than the "consciousness" of our everyday lives.

The term "Consciousness" is one most difficult to define adequately; and this quite naturally, for Consciousness can be defined and described only in the terms of its own experiences—there is no other term analogous to it which would serve to indicate it to one who had not experienced consciousness. The word which probably best expresses the general idea is the term "awareness."

The Rosicrucian teachings hold that Consciousness manifests on Seven Planes, each of which planes is interlinked with and blends into the one on either side of it (see figure illustrating the symbol). But each plane is composed of seven sub-planes, and each sub-plane of seven minor planes, and so on until the multiplication is made seven times. Each of the Seven Planes of Consciousness is named in the following synopsis of the teaching, and the main characteristics of each plane is given.

I. The Plane of the Elements

On this Plane of Consciousness is manifested the actions and reactions between the subtle elements of which all material forms are composed. Here occurs the play between the atoms, the electrons, the ions, the corpuscles, and the still more tenuous particles of substance of which science has as yet no knowledge. And, going still further back, it may be said that on this plane occurs the play of phases of substance as much more tenuous and subtle than the electrons as the latter are more tenuous than the atoms. Little can be said concerning these practically unknown forms and phases of matter, although the occult teachings are quite full of them.

In previous quotations from Haeckel, and other modern scientists, we have seen that advanced modern science recognizes the presence of ''something like consciousness'' in the atoms of matter, and ascribes their movements to ''likes and dislikes,'' ''loves and hates,'' arising from the perception of certain qualities in each other, and the response thereto: this means, of course, that the atoms possess and manifest ''feeling'' and ''will'' in an elementary form, phase, and degree. There are results arising from these manifestations of consciousness on the part of the atoms, however, which are not usually taken notice of by writers of the subject, either in the ranks of the occultists, or those of science. Let us now consider these, briefly.

Science informs us that all forms of physical energy or force, manifesting as light, heat, electricity, magnetism, etc., arise from vibrations of the particles of which matter is composed. These vibrations are, of course, caused by the motion of the particles; and these motions are caused by the manifestation of attraction or repulsion between the particles. Proceeding further, we see that the manifestation of attraction and repulsion between the particles of matter arise from the "likes and dislikes," the "loves and hates" of the atoms and particles—and that these, in turn are but **manifestations of elemental consciousness.** So we see, here, that even the manifestation of physical energy and force is but the accompaniment and result of the presence and activity of elemental consciousness.

On this plane of consciousness are operated many of those forms of "magic" known to all occultists. The occultist moves Matter not by exerting a physical force upon it by means of his mind and will, but, instead, by acting upon the consciousness of the material atoms by the power of his own consciousness! This is no place, of course, to go into detail concerning this phase of occultism, but it has been thought well to indicate here the source and nature of the power underlying occult phenomena of this kind, and the "why and wherefore" of its manifestation.

The Plane of Elemental Consciousness, like all the great Planes of Consciousness, contains seven subplanes, and each of these seven minor planes, and so on until the multiplication has been made seven times. The sub-plane we have just briefly considered is but one of the seven, and the remaining six are equally important. In these unmentioned subplanes there are manifestations utterly unknown to modern science and to the uninformed person, but of which the occult masters have made a careful and thorough study.

II.   The Plane of the Minerals

On this Plane of Consciousness are manifested the actions and reactions of the molecules of which the minerals are composed, and of the masses of mineral matter as well. Just as the atoms of matter manifest attraction and repulsion, arising from "like and dislike" of consciousness, so do the molecules of matter manifest a similar "like and dislike," resulting in the attraction and repulsion between molecules and masses of matter. The molecules or particles of which a piece of steel, for instance, is composed, hold together by reason of the attractive power of "cohesion," and not because they are "fastened together" by any mechanical means employed by nature. In the same way, gravitation manifests its attractive force.

Moreover, on some of the higher minor planes of this Plane of the Minerals, there is manifested the crystallization of the mineral particles according to a definite principle of design embedded in the consciousness of its particles. The crystal is built upon a definite plane, just as truly as is the acorn or the oak—and in all of these cases the pattern is but an "idea" in the consciousness of the combined particles. The Universal Builder works through the consciousness of the mineral particles just as truly and as wonderfully as through the particles of humanity which we call individual men. The study of crystals, and their formation will open up a new world of thought to the average person, and will give him a peep into the workshop of the Universal Builder in which he will see things heretofore unsuspected and undreamt.

The common opinion is that crystals are formed by mechanical causes, such as outside pressure, etc., but the careful student of science, as well as the occultist, knows that the formation of a crystal is a growth, and is as much the result of stored-up psychical ideas in the particles, as is the growth of plant substance or animal bodies. The student of crystallography soon becomes convinced of the presence of Life and Consciousness in the world of crystals.

In the contemplation of the Plane of Mineral Consciousness, the student must remember that there are forms of minerals far more gross than those visible to us on this earth; and also, that there are forms and phases of mineral life far finer and higher than those with which we are familiar here. The occult teachings contain some very interesting information concerning (these to us) unknown mineral forms and manifestation.

It may be mentioned here that the ancient alchemists (and some of the true modern alchemists) have found in the fact of mineral consciousness the missing-link of their science. The occultist having a comprehensive understanding of the consciousness of a metal or mineral will be able to work transformations upon and through it which would be impossible by means of chemistry or mechanical methods of treating metals. Here again, is given a passing hint regarding a subject of tremendous importance.

III. The Plane of the Plants

On this plane of Consciousness are manifested the actions and reactions of the protoplasmatic cells of which the plants are composed. And on this plane, as all the other planes of Consciousness, there are to be found high and low sub-planes and subdivisions of the latter.

At the lower pole of this plane we find plant-life which is scarcely distinguishable from the higher forms of mineral life—in fact, as we have seen previously, it is almost impossible to draw a fixed line separating the two great plane-divisions, for all planes blend into each other and are linked one with the other on the lower and higher poles of their activity. We have mentioned the Diatoms, or ''living crystals'' which the best authorities regard as the ''missing link'' between the two great kingdoms of Life and Consciousness, but which really are plants rather than minerals. The Diatoms belong to an order of flowerless plants, a genus of the Algols. They are covered by a silicious covering which gives them a crystalline appearance. They present the appearance of crystalline fragmentary particles, generally bounded by right lines, flat, stiff and brittle, usually nestling in slime in which they unite into various forms and combinations, and from which they often again separate. They multiply and reproduce themselves by division and conjugation.

In 1886, Professor Van Schrom, of Naples, Italy, was experimenting with the bacilli of the Asiatic cholera, and was examining the same under his high-power microscope. He was attracted by the formation of double pyramids of bacilli in the shape and general appearance of true crystals. These ''living crystals'' manifested growth and movement, and seemed to be alive and conscious. From these experiments he arrived at the conclusions that all bacteria produce living crystals, and his continued experiments seemed to verify his contention. These bacteria-crystals are composed of homogeneous albuminous matter, which at first is colorless and structureless, and which at a certain stage of their life history seem to lose their life qualities and to become, to all intents and purposes, "dead" crystals. These living crystals seem to be impelled by some inherent force akin to vital action to assume a geometrical figure. And while possessing these indications of elementary vegetable life they also exhibit the characteristic qualities of crystals, viz., refraction, inclusion, absorption, and polarization. Later investigations have revealed the presence of similar living crystals in the secretions of living organisms.

That Life is present in plant-life scarcely anyone is disposed to question, though there seems to be a desire to deny Consciousness and intelligent activity in the case on the part of the orthodox scientist. But the more advanced of the workers in the ranks of modern science do not hesitate to positively assert the presence of conscious intelligent activity in plant-life, and vigorously support their contention by logical argument backed up by incontrovertible facts gleaned in their laboratory experiments. These scientists hold that the presence of the phenomena of nutrition, reproduction, and of physical and chemical change due to adaptation is proof positive of the presence of vital intelligence within the organism in which the former are manifested.

Professor Bieser says: "**Adaptation,** after all, is the best evidence of the presence of intelligence or life in forms or units of matter. Adaptation, also called '**physiological** adaptation,' but best called '**psychological** adaptation,' is the one weapon by which living organisms fight against the destructive forces of conditions of nature. In all its forms, adaptation is the more or less successful co-operation of living organisms with the laws of nature—it is not the disregard of natural laws. In taking adaptation as our criterion by which the presence of intelligence is determined, we find no difficulty in settling the question of the presence of life. The most perfect automatic machinery has no life, because it cannot adapt itself in the least to the changing environmental conditions and thus save itself from annihilation, when necessity arises, by the performance of simple intelligent acts.''

In their consideration of the question of the presence of consciousness in the kingdom of plant-life, the writers divide the manifestations of intelligence into three classes, namely: **Trophoses,** or acts pertaining to nutrition; **Neuroses,** or acts pertaining to the nervous system; and **Psychoses,** or acts pertaining to thought processes.

The manifestation of Trophoses, or acts pertaining to nutrition, is apparent even in the case of the lowest forms of plant-life. Even the lowliest vegetable cell takes nourishment and replaces the waste products of its system by fresh material taken into its system. These activities require a very simple nervous system, often practically no nervous system at all. But, nevertheless, in every act of nutrition there is manifested not only the presence of Life, but also conscious activity of a certain degree. Even the lowest forms of plants are able to distinguish perfectly between nutritive and non-nutritive particles of matter. Most plants possess no nervous system, at least none yet discovered by science, but, nevertheless, they manifest characteristic Trophoses corresponding in degree with their necessities, but seldom exceeding those necessities.

Other plants, however, have a comparatively highly developed nervous system, or something corresponding to it, and manifest Neuroses, or acts pertaining to the nervous system, of a comparatively high degree. This is true of the "sensitive plants," and certain other plants of a high development in this direction. Some of the orchids, and a few other plants, manifest Neuroses indicating clearly the presence of consciousness and a degree of intelligent activity.

Still higher in the scale we find certain species of plants manifesting true Psychoses, or **acts pertaining to thought processes,** although the latter are of a comparatively low order as compared to those manifested by the higher forms of animal life. With this class of manifestation the average student is not so well informed, and, therefore, it has been thought well to direct your attention in the following pages to these fascinating phenomena of plant-life. We think that a careful consideration of the facts now about to be presented to the student will bring to him a clear realization of the presence of actual conscious activity in the kingdom of the plants, and will cause him to accept the statement of that eminent authority, Professor Bieser, who has said: "While we believe that the intelligence of man, animals and plants is essentially the same in kind, we know that it differs enormously in degree and form. Even among men this degree of intelligence varies, but this is because some individuals by nature see but a little more clearly their needs than others, and live under more favorable circumstances—that is all!"

Dr. J. E. Taylor, an authority on the subject of

plant-psychology says: "Perhaps one reason why plants are usually denied consciousness and intelligence is because in the structure of even the highest developed species we find no specialized nervous track along which sensations may travel, or where they can be registered as in the case of the ganglia and brains of the higher animals. But it should be remembered that none of the creatures sub-kingdom of the Protozoa (the lowest of the grand divisions of the animal kingdom) possess nervous structures, whilst many of the next more highly organized animal sub-kingdom, the Coelenterata, have no trace, and the rest but a feeble development. Yet we do not deny these lowly organized animals a dim and diffused consciousness, or even the possibility of their structures being so modified that they can profit by experience, and thus develop that accumulated experience of their kind that we call 'instinct.' "

Darwin, speaking of the wonderful sensitiveness of the root-tip of plants says: "It is hardly an exaggeration to say that the tip of the radicle thus endowed, and having the power of directing the movements of the adjoining parts, **acts like the brain of one of the lower animals**; the brain being seated within the anterior end of the body, receiving impressions from the sense organs, and directing the general movements." Professor Cope says: "We can understand how by parasitism, or other means of getting a livelihood without exertion, the adoption of new and skillful movements would become unnecessary, and consciousness itself would be seldom aroused. Continued repose would be followed by subconsciousness, and later by unconsciousness. Such appears to be the history of the entire vegetable kingdom.''

Dr. J. C. Arthur, in his interesting work entitled ''The Sagacity and Morality of Plants,'' says: ''I have tried to show that all organisms, even to the very simplest, whether plant or animal, from the very nature of life and the struggle for its maintenance, must be endowed with conscious feeling, pleasure and pain being its simplest expression. I have been told in Java, as one walks through a tangle of sensitive plants, they will drop down in their deprecating way for yards on either side, as if suddenly aroused into life, only to be again transformed into lifeless sticks by some unseen power. * * * The physical basis of life, Protoplasm, is the same for plants as for animals. The first differentiated or modified form of this we meet is the curious animalcule called Amoeba. As we watch its movements we cannot refrain from ascribing to it some dim consciousness of the life it leads. But amoeboid structure is common even in the lowest kinds of plants, and amoeboid movements can be seen in some of its tissues. Witness also the habits and intelligent movements of the zoospores of sea-weed and many other Algae, and the locomotion of the antherozoa of mosses, ferns, etc. Not many years ago these objects were classed as animals, and nobody doubted these so-called animals behaved consciously and intelligently. * * * Nothing can be more marked than the likes and dislikes of plants. Human beings can hardly express the same feelings more decidedly. There is perhaps even a 'messmateship' among plants, which inclines species to prefer to grow in company. Hosts of common plants perform actions which, if they were done by human beings, would at once be brought into the category of right and wrong. **There is hardly a virtue or a vice which has not its counterpart in the actions of the vegetable kingdom.** As regards conduct in this respect, there is small difference between the lower animals and plants.''

One of the most elementary manifestations of consciousnesss, and conscious action, in plant life is what has been called ''the gravity sense,'' or the sense by which the plant recognizes the ''up and down'' direction of growth. The germinating seed always sends its roots downward, no matter how the seed may be placed in the ground. This cannot be held to result merely from the action of gravitation, for the sprouts move upward and away from the centre of gravity just as truly as the roots move downward and toward it. Experiments have proven that this ''sense of direction'' is as much a true sense as that of any of the special senses of the lowly animal life-forms. The experiment has been tried of turning around a sprouting seed, the result being that in a day or so the roots will be again found to be turning downward and the sprouts turning upward. A French botanist, named Duhamel, once placed some beans in a cylinder filled with moist earth. After they had begun to sprout, he turned the cylinder a little to one side. The next day he turned it a little further in the same direction. Each day he would turn it a little more, until finally it had described several full circles. Then he took out the plant, and shaking off the clinging earth, he found that the beans' roots and sprouts had described circles—two perfectly formed spirals being shown, one of the tiny roots and the other of the tiny sprouts. The roots in their constant endeavor to move downward had formed one perfect spiral, while the sprouts in the constant effort to rise upward had described another perfect spiral. No amount of effort will cause the roots of a plant to grow upward, or its sprouts to grow downward. Each, root and sprout, has its own "sense of direction" to which it faithfully and invariably responds. In the same way, and from a similar cause, the tendrils of climbing plants will faithfully move toward the nearby support, and if they are untwined they will return during the next night to the old support, if possible. Moving pictures, carefully prepared, and taken over a long period, show that the movements of these tendrils to be akin to the movements of the limbs of an animal—the feelers and graspers of the octopus for example.

Not only have the roots of plants the general "sense of direction" which causes them to grow downward in spite of all attempts to prevent them, but they have also the "sense of moisture," which causes them to seek the direction of water. Many plants also turn their leaves and blossoms to the light, no matter how often they are turned in the opposite direction. Potatoes in dark cellars will often send forth their sprouts twenty or thirty feet in the direction of light which shows through a tiny crack in the wall. Likewise, plants possess the "sense of taste" to a very high degree in some cases. By means of this sense they are able to detect differences in substances, and to choose those substances which are conducive to their nutrition. They are able to distinguish between poor and rich soil, and also between different chemicals of differing nutritive values. They always move their roots in the direction of the best food supply, and also toward moisture. Not only do the roots of plants move in the direction of water, but instances have been cited in which the leaves of plants will bend over during the night and dip themselves in a vessel of water several inches away. Insect-eating plants recognize the difference between living animal substance and bits of inorganic matter or vegetable substance, casting off the latter two as if in disgust. Experiments have been made of placing a bit of cheese in the reach of such plants, when, though cheese is of course unfamiliar to them, they will seem to recognize its nitrogenous nature and will devour it as readily as they will a piece of flesh or the body of an insect.

Many students are doubtless familiar with the instance of the ''sensitive plants'' which exhibit a marked degree of sensibility to touch. Many insect-eating plants manifest an equally high degree of sensitiveness, though of course in a different direction. The leaves of the Venus' Fly Trap fold upon each other and thus capture the unfortunate insect which has been tempted into the trap by the sweet juice which appears upon the leaf as a dainty bait. The folding of the leaves follows the alarm given by the three sensitive bristles or hairs which act as **feelers** which sense the presence of the insects. Bits of earth, or raindrops, are recognized as ''not-food'' by these feelers, and no closing of leaves result from their presence on the leaves. Other plants are very sensitive to degrees of light, and they close at certain hours, the time varying according to the species of the plant. It was formerly held that this sensitiveness to light was merely a chemical response to the presence of light, but recent experiments have shown that such plants, when placed in a dark room, will continue this closing for several days, in a gradually lessening degree, thus indicating the presence of a "habit" within their consciousness, which "habit" indicates the presence of "mind" even more forcibly than does the closing itself. Certain ferns will wither if their fronds are touched too often.

In the case of seeds, the presence of consciousness and mental operations are manifested. Not only in the process of sprouting, but also in other processes, does the seed show signs of life and mind. Certain seeds are carried to their future abode by means of running streams along which they work their way to congenial soil by means of tiny projecting filaments which they move as legs, and thus propel themselves to shore. A botanist has said regarding a certain species of these "swimming seeds:" "So curiously lifelike are their movements that it is almost impossible to believe that these tiny objects, make good progress through the water, are really seeds and not insects."

Certain plants prey upon other plants, twining bands around another plant or tree, which bands work their way through the outer covering of the bark and thus act as suckers through which the parasitic plant draws nourishment from the larger plant, the latter succumbing in time and being literally killed for food by the clinging plant. In South America there are varieties of these climbers which will mount to the top of a tall tree in this way, and after killing their support they will wave long tendrils in the breeze until they fasten hold of another tree which in turn is depleted of its vitality and nourishment, and so on until the parasite is surrounded by a large circle of ruined victims. Other parasites content themselves with boring into a tree trunk and then absorbing enough of the sap of the latter to enable them to live without other work on their own part. In some species, the habit of parasitism is known to have been acquired during the history of the plant, just as some animals (and human beings) have acquired similar habits.

Other plants prey upon animals, and are equipped with mental faculties enabling them to efficiently capture their prey. We have typical illustrations of the adaptation of means to end in the case of the insect-eating plants previously referred to, but there are certain forms of plant-life which trap and devour much large animals; which forms are found principally in tropical countries. Dunstan, the naturalist, reported finding on the banks of Lake Nicaragua a particularly vicious plant of this class which by the natives is called the Devil's Noose. This bush-like plant is equipped with long tendrils, or whip-like feelers, flexible, strong, black, polished, and without leaves, which secrete a viscid fluid. These tendrils are employed by the plant to entangle small animals passing under its bush, and to then drain their blood and absorb their flesh. The naturalist one day passing along the banks of this lake was aroused by the shrieks and cries of his small dog. Pushing forward through the underbrush he found the little animal tightly enmeshed in a number of these black, slimy, bandlike tendrils which were cutting into its flesh by chafing and rubbing, the bleeding-point have been reached in a number of places. He found that these bands were the tendrils or branches of this particularly carnivorous plant, which he described as virtually "a land octopus." The natives of the tropics have weird legends of man-eating plants or trees of this kind, but so far science has not discovered an actual specimen of this kind, though it is admitted that the same is not beyond the bounds of possibility.

Other plants have roots which capture and kill small burrowing animals like moles, and then slowly absorb the nourishment from their blood and flesh. The plant kingdom has its Thugs and stranglers, as well as its vampires, according to the best authorities.

Professor Bieser says: "Another plant showing irritability when touched, and possessing the faculty of finding and raising water by means of a long, slender, flat stem or tube, is a variety of orchid discovered by E. A. Suverkrop, of Philadelphia, several years ago. This plant grows upon the trunks of trees hanging over swampy places along the bank of the Rio de la Plata and streams of the neighborhood. When this orchid is in want of water, the slender stem gradually unwinds until it dips into the water. Then the stem slowly coils around and winds up to discharge upon the part of the plant from which the roots spring the water which it has sucked up into its hollow space or tube within its interior. Sometimes when water is absent from directly under this plant, the stem moves first in this direction and then in another, in its search for water, and finally finding the water it performs the process above described. If this plant is touched while the stem is extended it acts much like the sensitive plant (mimosa), and the stem coils up into a spiral more rapidly than when it is lifting water."

The experiments of that wizard of plant-life, Luther Burbank, give us many illustrations of the manner in which the "mind" in the plant will respond to changed environment, and to take advantage of improved conditions thereof in the direction of adapting itself thereto. No one can study the works of modern botanists, or work long among plants, without discovering for himself many facts serving to prove that there is not only Life among the plants, but also sufficient mind to serve the purposes and needs of the existence of the plant. Some scientists have thought it possible that by changing the environment of the plant sufficiently, in the direction of calling out latent possibilities of mental action, it is probable that plants may be evolved which would approach in their mental activity that of the lower forms of animal life, if not indeed exceed the latter.

IV. The Plane of the Animals

Here, once more, we discover that there is no fixed dividing line between the adjoining Planes of Consciousness. Just as the Mineral Consciousness is closely blended into the Plant Consciousness, as we have seen, so is the Plant Consciousness closely blended into the Animal Consciousness. In fact, in the lowly forms of animal life it is almost impossible, at times, to state positively whether the particular form under consideration is a plant or an animal. Forms which science formerly considered ''animal'' are not placed in the category of ''plant-life;'' and other forms which science once held to belong to the plant-kingdom are now placed in the category of animal-life. The occultist recognized that these disputed forms dwell in the region in which the two respective planes blend and intermingle as has been stated before in these pages.

Consciousness in animal-life varies from the first faint glimmerings in the single-cell creatures in the slime of the ocean bed to the full dawn in the highest forms of animal-life like the horse, the dog, the elephant, etc. In each and every case, however, it will be found that each creature is endowed with a sufficient degree of intelligence to meet its needs and requirements—to adapt it to its environment. As the environment increases in complexity, the form of animal life has either adapted its consciousness to meet the requirements, or else has perished in the course of evolution.

Both science, and the occult teachings, inform us that animal life had its origin in the slime of the primeval ocean beds, and took the form of the "single cell" creatures. The best known form of single-cell animal is the Moneron (plural, monera), which is composed of but a single cell, and is like a tiny drop of glue. It belongs to the lowest class of animal-life, known as the Protozoa. The Moneron lives in water, and is a very minute shapeless, colorless, slimy, sticky, drop of protoplasmic substance. It has no organs of any kind, and all of its parts are similar—it lacks the separate organs or parts with which to perform the offices of the living creature as found in the higher forms of life. And yet this organless creature performs the processes of like known, respectively, as nutrition, reproduction, sensation, and will-action. Every part of the Moneron is capable of absorbing food and oxygen—it is all stomach and all lungs. Moreover, it is all reproductive organism. It envelops its prey by enclosing the latter as a drop of glue encloses a tiny gnat; and it then absorbs the nourishment from its food through every portion of its surface coming in contact with the food. It moves by prolonging a portion of itself outward, like a tiny tail or finger—this constitutes the "false foot" by which it propels, pushes, or pulls itself forward or backward, or sidewise. When it gets ready, it pulls back the "false foot" into its general substance, and is the same as before. It has no distinction of sex, but reproduces itself by simply growing larger and then dividing itself into two— and the process is over, there being two Monera where only one Moneron was the moment before. And yet this simple creature receives impressions from outside, and responds thereto. It seeks its food, and escapes its enemies. It has all the mind it needs.

Next in the rising scale of animal life we find the Amoeba. This creature also is a one-celled animal. It progresses by a continuous projection of "false feet" and a subsequent drawing-in of the same, which gives it the appearance of a many-fingered, or many-footed thing. This creature has the beginning of "parts" and "organs." In the first place it has a "nucleus" at its centre, and also an expanding and contracting cavity within itself which it uses for holding, digesting, and distributing its food—a rudimentary stomach, so to speak. It also has something like a "skin" on its surface, and it cannot be turned "inside out" like its brother the Moneron without disturbing its life.

Let us pause here for a moment, before passing on to the consideration of the higher forms of animal-life. The purpose of the pause is to call your attention to the resemblance of the Monera and the Amoebae to the cells of which the human body is composed. The ordinary cells of the higher animal, and mankind, closely resemble the Monera in many ways, while the white corpuscles of the blood of animals and men bear a striking resemblance to the Amoebae, so far as is concerned their size, general structure, and movements—in fact, science classes them as "amoeboids." The white corpuscles of our blood—these "amoeboids"—change their shape, take food in an intelligent manner, and live an apparently independent life, with movements showing undoubted "thought" and "will."

The cells of which the bodies of animals and men are composed are really independent living creatures, each of which is possessed of sufficient "mind" to enable it to perform its necessary life-work and offices. By means of the operation of what occultists know as the "group mind" by which a number of independent cells coordinate their activities, these cells perform the coordinated work of the organism. Each of these cell-minds manifests a perfect adaptation for its particular work. The work of those cells, in extracting from the blood the exact amount of nourishment needed by it, is but a minor evidence of the presence of such mind in them. The process of digestion, assimilation, etc., is another instance of the intelligence of the cells and cell-groups. In the healing of wounds, in which the cells rush to the points at which their services are needed, we have a striking instance of the selective intelligence of the cells. The cells of the body are constantly at work, performing the multitudinous offices of the organism, working separately, in small groups, and in great groups, according to the nature of the work to be done.

Some of the cells of the body are active workers, manufacturing the secretions and fluids needed in the varied work of the system. Others belong to "the reserves," and are kept under "waiting orders" awaiting the call to duty in the case of an accident or other emergency. Some are stationary, others remain stationary until they are called into motion to meet some requirement, others are constantly moving about, some making regular trips and others being rovers. Some of the moving cells perform the work of carriers, some move from place to place doing odd jobs, others perform scavenger work, and a large number are employed on the police-force of the body, or else constitute the cell-army.

The carrier cells—the red-corpuscles of the blood—travel in the arteries and veins, carrying a load of oxygen on the outward arterial trip, and bringing back a return cargo of the waste products of the system to be burned up in the lungs. Other cells force their way through the walls of the arteries and veins, and through the tissues of the body, on repair work. The police cells, and the soldier-cells, in the blood protect the system from the attacks of germs, bacteria, and other harmful visitors or invaders. One of the protecting cells coming in contact with an intruder of this kind will enmesh it, and then proceed to devour it; if the task be too heavy for one cell it will call the assistance of others, and the combined force will seize the intruder and try to eject it from the system.

The work of the cells in repairing a wound furnishes one of the most striking in illustrations of the presence of intelligence in the cells. When a portion of the body is wounded, it is found that the tissues, lymphatic and blood vessels, glands, muscles, nerves, and sometimes even the bone are severed. The alarm is sounded by the nervous system, and the repair-cells rush to the spot in great numbers. The flowing blood washes away the dirt and foreign substances—or at least endeavors to do so. Then the blood coagulates and forms a scab to protect the wound. By this time millions of blood cells have arrived on the scene, and the repair work begins at once. The cells display the most wonderful activity and intelligence in this work. The cells of the tissues, nerves, blood-vessels, etc., on each side of the wound begin to reproduce themselves very rapidly, and gradually form a bridge over the space between the two sides of the wound, bringing each side together. In this bridge work they display intelligence, purpose and system. The cells of the blood-vessels connect with the same kind of cells on the opposite side of the wound, forming new tubes through which the blood may flow. The cells of the connective tissues do likewise, and so do the cells of each of the other kinds of bodily substance. Then after the "inside work" is complete, new epidermis cells form a new skin over the healed wound. The above gives you but a passing glimpse of the wonderful intelligent work of the cells in performing their offices in the body—what has not been told is equally as wonderful. To all intents and purposes the cells of the body are like the individual bees in the hive, i. e., intelligent, independent living creatures working together for the common good.

The above digression was made in order to acquaint you with the wonderful intelligence which is possible of manifestation by the counterparts of the Monera and the Amoebae—those lowly forms of one-cell life which we have been considering on the preceding pages. An understanding of the facts above related will bring home to each student the full perception and appreciation of the truth of the statement previously made, i. e., that **each living creature, from highest to lowest, is endowed with a degree of consciousness and intelligence proportionate to its requirements in its life-work and activities.**

Some of the Amoebae—the Diatoms, for instance—secrete solid matter from the water, and build themselves tiny houses or shells to protect themselves from their enemies. These shells have tiny openings through which the creature may project its "false feet" for purposes of movement, and for securing food. The skeletons of these minute creatures form the deposits of chalk found in many parts of the world.

Next higher in the scale come the Infusoria, which are distinguished by having tiny vibrating filaments, or thread-like appendages, which they employ for purposes of motion and grasping their food. These filaments are permanent, and are the beginning of the manifestation of permanent limbs in the animal world. These elementary creatures have also evolved rudimentary mouth-openings, and also a short gullet which is a rudimentary throat, windpipe, and food-passage.

Then come the Sponges, slimy creatures employing a spongy, soft skeleton (the latter being what we commonly call "sponges"). This creature also employs whip-like filaments with which to gather its food. Then come the Polyps, which fasten themselves to floating objects, mouth downward, with tentacles serving to seize their food. The Jellyfishes which belong to this family also have rudimentary muscles, the contraction of which enables the creature to "swim." They also possess a rudimentary nervous system, and rudimentary eyes and ears. Next in the ascending scale come the Star-Fish, Sea-Urchin, and their kind, some of which possess a well defined nervous system, a true stomach, and eyes. Then come the Annulosa, or jointed creatures, comprising the various families of Worms, Crabs, Spiders, Ants, etc. This great family of creatures comprises nearly four-fifths of the known life-forms of the animal kingdom. Their bodies are well formed, and they have quite well-developed nervous systems, eyes, and other sense organs, and in some of the higher forms a circulatory system distributing a fluid akin to blood, which distributes the blood and oxygen to all parts of the body of the creature. Highest in the scale of this great family are the Insects, with their many varieties, the characteristics of which need not be described here, all being familiar with them. The wonders of spider-life, of ant-life, of bee-life, have been depicted by great naturalists, and the student will need no additional assurance of the presence of intelligence within the being of these tiny creatures and their relations in the insect world. Darwin once said that ''the brain of the ant, although not much larger than a pin-point, is one of the most marvelous atoms of matter in the world, perhaps more so than the brain of man.'' Then come the Mollusca, which group includes the oyster, clam, snail, etc. Some of the higher forms of this family show signs of a rudimentary vertebra, and may be considered as possibly the ''connecting link'' between the invertebrates and the Vertebrates.

Next in the ascending scale come the Vertebrates, so called by reason of the presence in them of a vertebra or spinal column, or ''backbone,'' and an **internal** skeleton as contrasted with the external skeleton of the lower forms of life. At the lowest end of the scale of the vertebrates are found the great family of Fishes, with high and low species. Then come the Reptiles, with its species of snakes, lizards, turtles, crocodiles, etc. There are many ''connecting links'' between the family of Fishes and that of the Reptiles; and also many between the family of Reptiles, and the family of Birds which is next highest in the scale. Among the birds, particularly in the Crow family, we find examples of a high degree of intelligence.

Next above the Birds come the Mammals, which is connected with the family of Birds by several strange "connecting links"—for instance the Australian Duck-Bill, which strange creature lays eggs, and then when her eggs are hatched nourishes them with milk from her breast. In the great family of Mammals, are the following sub-families of animals, viz.: The **Monotremes**, or half-bird, half-mammal creatures; the **Marsupials**, or milk-giving, pouched animals, which carry their imperfectly developed young in an extended pouch until maturity—such as the opossum and kangaroo; the **Placentals**, or creatures having the placenta or appendage through which the young is nourished in the womb before birth—that is the Royal Line through which the higher forms of the Mammals proceeded.

Among the **Placentals**, are found the following sub-families: The **Edentata**, or toothless creatures, such as the sloths, ant-eaters, armadillos, etc.; the **Sirena**, or sea cows, manatess, dugongs, etc.; the **Cetacea**, or whales, dolphins, porpoises, etc., which resemble fishes but which are true mammals, bringing forth matured young which are nourished at the breast; the **Ungluta**, or hoofed animals, such as the horse, the cow, the rhinoceros, the hippopotamus, the pig, the camel, the deer, the sheep, etc.; the **Hyracoidea**, or family of the coney, rock, rabbit, etc.; the **Proboscidea**, or trunked animals, such as the elephants; the **Carnivora**, or flesh-eaters, including the seal, the bear, the dog, the wolf, the lion, the tiger, the leopard, etc. The wolf and similar animals belong to the sub-family of dogs; while the lion, tiger, and similar animals belong to the sub-family of cats; the **Rodentia,** or gnawers, including the rat, the hare, the beaver, the squirrel, the mouse, etc.; the **Insectivora,** or insect-feeders, such as the mole, the shrew, the hedgehog, etc.; the **Cheiroptera,** or wing-fingered animals, including the great families of bats, etc.; the **Lemuroidea,** or Lemur family, the individuals of which resemble a monkey in general appearance, but have in addition a long bushy tail and a sharp muzzle like a fox—they are like a small fox having hands and feet like a monkey; the **Primates,** or family of creatures like the monkey, babboon, man-apes, gibbons, gorillas, chimpanzees, orang-outang, and finally, the "connecting links" between the apish forms and Man.

In this ascending scale of animal life the student will perceive countless varieties and species, sub-species and variations among species. And in each there will be perceived some slight difference in the degree and quality of the intelligence manifested by the creature. Even among the individuals of the same species there is found a great variation in such manifestations. But throughout it all, there is perceived to be a certain general plane of consciousness which may be called "The Animal Plane" as distinguished from "The Mineral Plane" on the one hand, and "The Human Plane" on the other hand.

The Plane of the Human

Passing from the Plane of Animal Consciousness to that of the Plane of Human Consciousness, we soon become cognizant of the presence of a new element of consciousness. This element is known as "Self Consciousness," or the consciousness which enables Man to say, knowingly, of himself "I am

I''—to identify himself as the Thinker, apart from the thoughts; the Actor apart from the action; the Feeler, apart from the feelings; the Willer, apart from the voluntary activities; the Conscious Subject, apart from the phenomena of the senses. It is true that in the primitive forms of human life this new consciousness exists but as a faint dawn, but it is latent there; and as the ascent of Man progresses this new conscious flames out in higher and still higher forms. What this new element of Self-Consciousness is, we shall see presently.

In thinking of Man, we must remember that primitive human beings—little removed from the apes—are as much Man as is the highest individual of the race today, or as will be his still higher descendant of tomorrow. And we must not forget that the Plane of Human Consciousness is closely linked to, and blended with, the Plane of Animal Consciousness, at one of its sides. The best scientific, and the best occult teaching hold that the man and the ape descended from some common ancestral form in the long ages past; the common ancestor was the trunk from which the Man branch sprung on one side and the ape branch sprung on the other.

It must not be forgotten that the lowest races of Man known to us today are as far removed in degree of intelligence from the highest known types of mankind as from the highest apes or man-apes. In fact, many think that evolution from the highest apes to the Kaffir, Hottentot, or Digger Indian is no more difficult than would be the evolution of those lowly types of human life up to the types of Emerson, Shakespeare, Huxley, Darwin, Edison and other high types of cultured man. Huxley has shown us that the brain structure of Man as compared with the

Chimpanzee shows differences but slight as compared to the differences between that of the Chimpanzee and that of the Lemur. He also shows us that in the important feature of the deeper brain-furrows, and intricate convolutions, the chasm between the highest civilized man and the lowest savage is far greater than between the lowest savage and the highest man-ape. Darwin, in his description of the very low type of human beings found among the Fuegian savages, says: "Their very signs and expressions are less intelligible to us than those of the domesticated animal. They are men who do not possess the instinct of those animals, nor yet appear to boast of human reason, or at least of the arts consequent upon that reason."

Professor Clodd, in his description of the Primitive Man says: "Doubtless he was lower than the lowest of the savages of today—a powerful, cunning biped, with keen sense organs always sharper, by virtue of constant exercise, in the savage than in the civilized man (who supplements them by science), strong instincts, uncontrolled and fitful emotions, small faculty of wonder, and nascent reasoning power; unable to forecast tomorrow, or to comprehend yesterday, living from hand to mouth on the wild products of Nature, clothed in skin and bark, or daubed with clay, and finding shelter in trees and caves; ignorant of the simplest arts, save to chip a stone missile, and perhaps to produce fire; strong in his needs of life and vague sense of right to it and to what he could get, but slowly impelled by common perils and passions to form ties, loose and haphazard at the outset, with his kind, the power of combination with them depending on sounds, signs and gestures."

The consideration of that characteristic phase of

Consciousness known as the Self-Consciousness of Man will be pursued further in the succeeding chapter, in which chapter will also be taken up the consideration of the two still higher Planes of Consciousness known as "The Plane of the Demi-Gods," and "The Plane of the Gods," respectively.

PART VIII

THE THREE HIGHER PLANES OF CONSCIOUSNESS

We have now reached that stage of our presentation of the subject of the Secret Doctrine of the Rosicrucians, and particularly of that phase known as the Seven Planes of Consciousness, in which we ask the student to consider those phases of Consciousness above the Plane of Animal Consciousness. Accordingly our present consideration is with those three great Planes of Consciousness which begin with the Plane of Human Consciousness, and include the Planes of the Consciousness of the Demi-Gods, and which find their highest manifestation on the Plane of the Consciousness of the Gods.

While these three higher Planes of Consciousness are included in the Rosicrucian symbol of the seven Planes of Consciousness, i. e., the seven linked circles, the Rosicrucians have also a special symbol by which they seek to indicate these three wonderful higher Planes of Consciousness, viz.: the symbol of the three linked circles (see illustration). It will be noticed here, also, that each of the circles are linked with the two on either side of it,—the circumference of each circle extending over that of the two others on either side of it; this indicates that each Plane of Consciousness is blended with the others, a truth which will be made more apparent as we progress without commentary on the teaching in this chapter.

V.   The Plane of Human Consciousness

The Plane of Human Consciousness, as its name indicates, is that plane of conscious activity which is manifested by human beings, high and low, in varying degrees.   This Plane of Consciousness, like all the others of the Seven Planes of Consciousness, is divided into seven sub-planes, and each of these

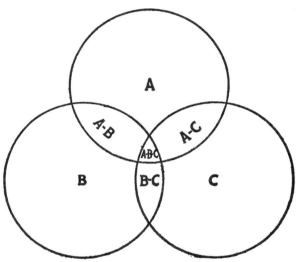

Figure 11.   Symbol of the Three Higher Planes of Consciousness

into seven, and so on, as explained in preceding chapters of this book.   Moreover, at one pole this plane is linked with, and blends into the highest sub-planes of the Plane of Animal Consciousness; while at its other pole it blends into the lower sub-planes of the next highest plane, i. e., the Plane of the Consciousness of the Demi-Gods.   Again, following the symbol of the Three Linked Circles, the same individual who manifests on the Plane of Human Consciousness is (in a measure) in touch with the two higher planes, known, respectively, as the Plane of the Consciousness of the Demi-Gods, and the Plane of Consciousness of the Gods.

The reason that the Rosicrucians place these three higher planes of consciousness in a trinity of circles, apparently apart from the lower four planes, is that on these three higher planes of consciousness the individual soul manifests Self-Consciousness, or the consciousness of "I Am," in at least a certain degree; while on the lower four planes this consciousness of "I" is entirely absent, and the mental activity is more or less automatic and instinctive. This distinction will be brought out as we proceed.

On the very lowest forms of Human Consciousness, the man's mental and emotional activity is but little more than that of the higher animals—in fact, in some cases the animals actually seem to display a greater degree of intellectual power, though on instinctive lines. But even in the lowest forms of human life there appears at least a faint glimmering of Self-Consciousness, or the conviction that "I Am I," that form of consciousness by means of which the human individual becomes aware of himself as an individual entity. This, rather than the degree of intellectual development, is the characteristic distinguishing mark of the human being.

It is quite difficult to describe clearly in words the actual distinction between the highest forms of animal consciousness, and the lowest forms of the self-consciousness of the human being, although the difference between the highest animal and the highest man in this respect is quite marked. Admitting the difficulty of the explanation, it may be said that while even in the case of the highest animal the consciousness is always directed **outward,** in even the lowest type of man there is at least a faint degree of the **inward** direction of consciousness. The animal always thinks of **outside** things, while even the primitive man occasionally thinks of **himself**—makes himself the object of his own thoughts, in at least the sense of considering his own feelings, ideas, etc., and comparing them with others previously had by him. Or again, there is no "inside world," or "something within," to the animal; while man always (at least in some degree) is aware of the "inside world," or the "something within" as distinguished from the "something without."

A favorite illustration of the psychologists, employed by them to point out the distinction between the "simple consciousness" of the higher animal, and the "self consciousness" of the human being is stated by a writer as follows: "A horse standing out in the cold sleet and rain undoubtedly feels the discomfort, and possibly the pain, for we know by observations that the animals feel both. But the horse is not able to analyze his mental states and to wonder when his master will come out to him; or to think how cruel it is to keep him out of the warm stable; or to wonder whether he will be taken out in the cold again tomorrow; or to feel envious of other horses who are indoors; or to wonder why he is compelled to be out on cold nights, etc., etc.—just as a man would do under the same circumstances. He is aware of the discomfort, just as is the man and he would run home if he could, just as would the man. But he is not able to pity himself, nor to think about his individuality or his personality, as would the man—nor does he wonder whether such a life is worth living, after all. He 'knows,' but does not 'know that he knows,' as does the man. The animal cannot 'know himself.' "

But we must not fall into the error of supposing that the primitive man, or even the less-developed individuals of modern civilization, possess this faculty of self-conscious to a high degree. On the contrary, with both of these types this form of consciousness may be said to exist merely in a "dawn state"—and yet the "dawn" is a distinct advance upon the darkness of the mental night. A modern psychologist says of the comparatively higher forms of self-consciousness: "Many persons never have more than a misty idea of such a mental attitude. They always take themselves for granted, and never turn the gaze inward."

The development of the higher forms of self-consciousness may be noted in the gradual unfoldment of the mind of the young child—for on the mental, as well as on the physical plane, the young of the human being rapidly passes through and reproduces the stages of the evolution of its ancestral forms. At a certain stage of the mental evolution or development of the young child there comes a particular period at which the child seems to awaken to a dawning realization that it is an individual, instead of being merely a bunch of feelings and desires. Up to a certain point the young child speaks of itself in the third person, i. e., as "Johnny," "Mary," etc. Then all of a sudden it begins to employ the terms "I" or "Me" in speaking of itself—though it may make grammatical errors in using these pronouns, nevertheless, there is never any doubt left that the child knows just what they stand for: it knows "I am I."

Some psychologists call attention to the fact that

many children experience a feeling of something akin to terror when they first reach this sense of "I," or individuality. Some writers have testified to having felt a strange sense of Aloneness, and detachment from all other things, when this sense of individuality first burst upon them in early childhood. In some cases the fuller dawn of self-consciousness is accompanied by a newly developed bashfulness, shyness, or that more or less morbid state known by the common name "self conscious." With the faculty of introspection, there often comes the tendency to employ the same too freely, and thus to become morbid on the one hand, or else foolishly egotistical and vain on the other hand.

A writer well says of this particular state of newly awakened consciousness: "Although this feeling of separateness and apartness grows less acute as the man grows older, yet it is always present to a greater or less degree until a still higher stage is reached, when it disappears. And this self-conscious stage is painful to many. Many find themselves entangled in a mass of mental states which one thinks is himself, or inextricably bound up with himself, and the struggle between the awakening Ego and its confining sheaths is very painful in some cases. And this becomes more painful as the individual advances in self-consciousness and nears the end at which he is to find deliverance. Man eats of the Tree of Knowledge and begins to suffer, and is driven out of the garden of Eden of the child consciousness in which the individual has lived like the birds, concerning not himself about the affairs of his higher nature. Man pays dearly for the gift of Self-Consciousness—yet it is worth it all, for finally he reaches heights of higher consciousness and is delivered from his burden.''

With the dawning awareness of one's own mental states, one comes to the realization that other human beings possess similar states, and one begins to speculate and reason about the working of these states in others. Then comes the desire to communicate one's ideas to the mind of the others, and to appeal to his feelings or reason. All this promotes the development of Intellect and logical thought, which is a marked characteristic of evolving human consciousness. Man begins to seek for an answer to the many "whys" which are presenting themselves to him, and he seeks to reason from the known to the unknown. He proceeds to invent appliances conducive to the accomplishment of things which he desires. He harnesses his Intellect to the chariot of his Desires, and drives it along by command of Will, the chariot-driver.

Man, indeed, pays a price for this advanced consciousness, as we have said. He pays a constantly increasing price as he advances into the new territory of conscious existence and experience. The more he knows, the more he desires; and the more he desires, the more does he suffer from the pain of not having. Capacity for pain is the price man pays for his advance in the scale; but he has a corresponding capacity for pleasure accompanying it. He has not only the pain of unsatisfied desires for possession of material things, and physical wants, but also the pain arising from the lack of intelligent answers to the ever-increasing volume of problems presenting themselves for solution to his evolving intellect; and he also has pain of unsatisfied longings, disappointments, frustrated aims and ambitions, and all the rest of the list.

The animal lives its life and is contented—for it knows no better. If it has enough to eat, a place to sleep, a mate, it is satisfied, and asks no more—it has few needs, and, while its degree of happiness is not great, it lacks the capacity for mental and emotional pain possessed by those higher in the scale. And many men are but little above this stage—they are easily satisfied; they are ignorant of the unsatisfied desires which render others unhappy. They have no unanswered questions—they do not even dream of the existence of such questions. But as man progresses, his wants multiply, and his pain increases. New wants are but partly satisfied, and the unsatisfied remainder bring pain to him. Civilization becomes more and more complex, and new wants and lacks manifest themselves. Man attaches himself to "things," and creates for himself artificial wants which he must labor to meet. His intellect often fails to lead him upward, and too often merely enables him to invent new and subtle means and ways of gratifying his senses in a way impossible to the animals or primitive man. Some men make a religion of the gratification of their sensuality and their appetites, and sink below the level of the beasts in this respect. Others become vain, conceited, and filled with an inflated sense of the importance of their personality. Others become morbidly introspective, and spend their time analyzing and dissecting their moods, motives, and feelings. Others exhaust their capacity for pleasure and happiness, by looking outside of themselves for happiness, instead of within. These are the dark shadows cast by the bright light of Human Consciousness, however

—the shadows always found as the "opposite" of all real evolutionary progress.

As man progresses in the scale of Self Consciousness, however, he finds himself gradually detaching his sense of the Self from its sheaths and working tools. He begins to realize that there is an "I Am" within his being, to which all the feelings, the emotions, the desires, and even the thoughts and ideas, are but incidents. In this high stage he perceives himself to be an "I Am" surrounded by his mental and emotional tools and belongings—a Sun surrounded by its whirling worlds and activities. He realizes that the Ego is not only superior to the body, but also to the "mind" and feelings; and he learns now only how to master and intelligently use his body, but also how to intelligently master and use his Intellect and his Emotions.

A well known writer has said of Man in this advanced stage: "If we are willing to believe in this mastery over the body, we must be prepared to believe in the mastery over our own inner thoughts and feelings. That a man should be a prey to any thought that chances to take possession of his mind is commonly among us assumed as unavoidable. It may be a matter of regret that he should be kept awake all night from anxiety as to the issue of a lawsuit on the morrow, but that he should have the power of determining whether he should be kept awake or not seems an extravagant demand. The image of an impending calamity is no doubt odious, but its very odiousness (we say) makes it haunt the mind all the more pertinaciously and it is useless to expel it.

"Yet this is an absurd notion—for man, the heir of all the ages: hag ridden by the flimsy creatures of his own brain. If a pebble in our boots torments us, we expel it. We take off the boot and shake it out. And once the matter is fairly understood it is just as easy to expel an intruding and obnoxious thought from the mind. About this there ought to be no mistake, no two opinions. The thing is obvious, clear and unmistakable. It should be as easy to expel an obnoxious thought from the mind as it is to shake a stone out of your shoe; and till a man can do that it is just nonsense to talk about his ascendancy over Nature, and all the rest of it. He is a mere slave, and prey to the bat-winged phantoms that flit through the corridors of his own brain. Yet the weary and careworn faces that we meet by thousands, even among the affluent classes of civilization, testify only too clearly how seldom this mastery is obtained. How rare indeed to meet a man. How common rather to discover a creature hounded on by tyrant thoughts (or cares or desires), cowering, wincing under the lash—or perchance priding himself to run merrily in obedience to a driver that rattles the reins and persuades him that he is free—whom we cannot converse with in a careless tete-a-tete because that alien presence is always there, on the watch.

"It is one of the most promising doctrines of certain schools of occult philosophy that the power of expelling thoughts, or if need be, killing them dead on the spot, **must** be attained. Naturally the art requires practice, but like other arts, when once acquired there is no mystery or difficulty about it. And it is worth practice. It may indeed fairly be said that life only begins when this art has been acquired. For obviously when, instead of being ruled by individual thoughts, the whole flock of them in their immense multitude and variety and capacity is ours to direct and dispatch and employ where we list, life becomes a thing so vast and grand compared with what it was before, that its former condition may well appear almost antenatal. If you can kill a thought dead, for the time being, you can do anything with it that you please. And therefore it is that this power is so valuable. And it not only frees a man from mental torment (which is nine-tenths at least of the torments of life), but it gives to him a concentrated power of handling mental work absolutely unknown to him before. The two things are correlative to each other.

"While at work your thought is to be actually concentrated in it, undistracted by anything whatever irrelevant to the matter in hand—pounding away like a great engine, with giant power and perfect economy—no wear and tear of friction, or dislocation of parts owing to the working of different forces at the same time. Then when the work is finished, if there is no more occasion for the use of the machine, it must stop equally, absolutely—stop entirely—no **worrying** (as if a parcel of boys were allowed to play their devilments with a locomotive as soon as it was in the shed)—and the man must retire into that region of his consciousness where his true self dwells. I say that the power of the thought-machine itself is enormously increased by this faculty of letting it alone on the one hand, and of using it singly and with concentration on the other. It becomes a true tool, which a master-workman lays down when done with, but which only a bungler carries about with him all the time to show that he is the possessor of it."

If the student will master the idea expressed in the above several quoted paragraphs, he will indeed become a Master of Mind. And if he will extend the idea to the field of his Emotions, and will put into practice there the same idea and method, he will also become a Master of his Emotions—an accomplishment of inestimable value. But, before doing either of these things he will find it necessary to come to a full realization of the fact that his Self—his real "I" —is a Something superior to and transcending both his Thought and his Emotions. He must enter into a vivid realization of the "I AM," before he may hope to be able to say "I Do" regarding these accomplishments. As the old Rosicrucian masters were wont to say: "When the 'I' knows itself to be the Self and Master, then only is it able to take its throne and enforce its will upon its subjects in the world of its thoughts, desires, feelings, and emotions."

Not only may the enlightened "I" manifest its power along the lines above indicated, but it may also work its will in that region which popular modern psychology has chosen to call "The Sub-Conscious Mind." The latter is merely that great region of mind outside of the limits of the concentrated field of attention. In that great region a great part of the thinking of the average man is performed, the results being flashed into the field of his attention in a more or less haphazard way. Without going deeply into the subject, we would say here that the man who has grasped the reality and power of the "I" is able to issue positive commands to this part of his mental machinery, and not only cause it to perform the work of thought classification, induction and deduction, for him, but also to present the report of such work to his conscious attention at any specified time and place. The Masters of Mind relieve themselves of much of the drudgery of ordinary intellectual processes in this way, and obtain results logically perfect and ready for use, according to the measure of training and direction which they have been able to impose upon the aforesaid regions of their mind.

In conclusion, it should be called to the attention of the student that the average man ''consciouses'' only on some of the lower subplanes and subdivisions of The Plane of Human Consciousness; and that there are wonderful regions within that great plane awaiting the exploration of the wise of the race, and the generations of the distant future. The wise of the race are not waiting for the centuries-long slow evolution of the bulk of the race, but are taking the ''short cut'' to the higher sub-planes by means of careful training along the lines indicated by capable teachers who have demonstrated the virtue and value of the methods which have been known to and taught by the advanced occultists for thousands of years, the Rosicrucian Teachings being splendid examples of such achievements.

Even without calling upon the two still higher Planes of Consciousness, the enlightened race may reach heights of mental achievement which are so far above those dreamed of by the average person of the race as to appear like the wildest fiction.

VI. The Plane of the Consciousness of the Demi-Gods.

There is a Plane of Consciousness so much higher than even the Plane of Human Consciousness—of even the highest sub-planes of that great plane— that the Rosicrucians have applied to it the somewhat fanciful term of ''The Plane of Consciousness of the Demi-Gods.'' This, because the individual who attains these heights, and is able to "conscious" on this plane is so much higher than mere Man that he seems to be "almost as the gods." The Rosicrucians teach that on this high plane of being dwell certain very advanced souls—once men, but now almost as gods when compared to men— who aid in the great work of the advancement of the race of men in the general course of spiritual evolution.

The teaching is that the race as a whole is slowly evolving on to the said higher Plane of Consciousness, and long ages from now will "conscious" normally on it. In the meantime, however, certain advanced souls have transcended the Human Plane, and have passed on to the higher plane, where they aid and assist the rest of the race. Moreover, to the individual whose unfoldment is rapid, from one or more of many well-known causes, there come at times "flashes of consciousness" from the higher plane aforesaid, which at least for the time being bring the individual into conscious contact with that plane. The pages of the mystic records are filled with statements of experiences of this kind. In certain forms of poetic fervor, religious exaltation, and mystic experience, these flashes come and are then recorded by the individual experiencing them—the record, however, usually being given in the terms of the philosophy, religion, or general belief of the person experiencing the contact or "illumination," the person not fully realizing from just what source the flash of Truth has come.

In recent years many of these experiences have been classified and included in works of writers, under the general name of "Cosmic Consciousness." In most cases the persons having attained these experiences, and those who have recorded them, are of the opinion that the flash of consciousness realized is the highest possible. But, as wonderful as are these experiences, they are in most cases but flashes of insight of the light of some of the lower sub-planes of the great Plane of the Demi-Gods—countless higher planes being existent and awaiting the unfoldment of being to experience their light and glory, and beyond all of such there existing the highest plane of all, the Plane of the Gods, to which all the rest is as but a faint shadow of the reality.

The characteristic feature of the Plane of Consciousness of the Demi-Gods is that of Oneness with Universal Life—the consciousness of the Life of All-Manifestation. Varying in many degrees and forms, of course, this is the characteristic feature of all experiences of this great plane of conscious activity. On this plane, the individual feels in close touch with all the rest of Creation—a united part of (not apart from) the ALL. The experience of even a slight momentary contact with this plane of being constitutes the common "mystic experience," of which sages, seers, poets, and illumined souls of all ages have sung, and regarding which they have tried to inform us in words inadequate to the task. The study of these mystic reports throw much light on the subject, and is well worth the time and attention of all true students of the Rosicrucian teaching. But the student must always remember that these experiences are not the end of all thought on the subject, nor the final word of Truth. As valuable as is this part of the teaching, it must never be mistaken for the highest peak of the Mountain of Truth.

To those who have experienced the flashes of

Illumination, or the glimpse of the Fire of Cosmic Consciousness—both of which classes of phenomena belong to the Plane of the Consciousness of the Demi-Gods—there has come a realization of the actual Oneness of Life in the Universe, and an actual awareness that the Universe is animated by One Life which is diffused among and permeates every portion of its extent and manifestation. To such has come an assurance that there is nothing "dead" in the Universe —that every part and portion, individual and collective, is instinct with Life. Not only this, but for at least the time of the experience there has come a sense of absolute certainty that the individual is in touch with this One Life, and is an actual centre of activity within its presence.

It should be pointed out, moreover, that in such experiences there is not merely the intellectual conviction of the certainty of the facts just stated, but that, on the contrary, there is manifested an actual "knowing," direct and immediate, of such facts. The person having the experience **knows** these things just as he knows that he himself is alive and present in the universe. It is impossible to convey the exact nature of this consciousness to any who have not had at least a faint flash of it. It can be described only in its own terms.

In most of these cases, while the actual consciousness has passed away after a few moments, there has been left a memory which abides ever with the individual, and which gives to him such a certainty of the truth of which he has been a witness that nothing can ever shake his conviction thereof. It must be remembered that these flashes of consciousness are prophecies of the stage of consciousness which at some future time will become the normal state of consciousness of the race. Moreover, it must not be forgotten that there exist certain advanced souls on this earth to whom this stage or state of consciousness is the normal and habitual one—and in whom there always exists a realization in actual consciousness of At-One-Ment with the Universal Life. Such beings are indeed Demi-Gods, as compared to the average human being. Some of the great world leaders—the founders of great religions, and others of their kind, were filled with this consciousness and strove to make it manifest in a veiled form to their followers who were not strong enough to bear the full truth. Many of these great souls are still present on the earth-plane in the flesh, in newly incarnated forms, continuing their work and striving to uplift the race.

A modern poet expressing the conviction of Universal Oneness of Life uses terms which will be recognized by all who have had flashes of Cosmic Consciousness, as follows:

"For the All is One, and all are part,
    And not **apart** as they seem to be;
And the blood of Life has a single heart,
    Beating through God, and clod, and Me!"

Walt Whitman, who himself had experienced Cosmic Consciousness, says of the experience:

"As in a swoon, one instant
Another sun, ineffable, full dazzles me,
And all the orbs I knew, and brighter, unknown orbs,
One instant of the future land, Heaven's land."
*   *   *   *   *   *   *   *   *   *
"I cannot be awake, for nothing looks to me as it
    did before,

Or else I am awake for the first time, and all before
   has been a mean sleep.

*   *   *   *   *   *   *   *   *

"When I try to tell the best I find, I cannot;
My tongue is ineffectual on its pivots,
My breath will not be obedient to its organs,
I become a dumb man."

Tennyson, according to his friends had glimpses
and flashes of Cosmic Consciousness, and in many
of his poems he has given expression to the thoughts
and feelings which had come to him at that time.
The following is a good illustration of the latter:

"For knowledge is the swallow on the lake
That sees and stirs the surface-shadow there,
But never yet hath dippt into the abysm,
The Abysm of all Abysms, beneath, within
The blue of sky and sea, the green of earth,
And in a million-millionth of a grain
Which cleft and cleft again for evermore
And ever vanishing, never vanishes   * * *
And more, my son, for more than once when I
Sat all alone, revolving in myself
That word which is the symbol of myself,
The mortal symbol of Self was loosed,
And passed into the Nameless, as a cloud
Melts into Heaven. I touched my limbs, the limbs
Were strange, not mine—and yet no shadow of doubt,
But utter clearness, and through loss of Self
The gain of such large life as matched with ours
Were Sun to spark, unshadowable in words,
Themselves but shadows of a shadow-world."

Dr. Richard Maurice Bucke, of Toronto, Canada,
a number of years ago published a book entitled

"Cosmic Consciousness," in which he grouped together a number of very interesting experiences along these lines which had been related by those experiencing them; Dr. Bucke himself, as well as his friend Walt Whitman, and several other close friends, had experienced flashes of this same stage of consciousness. He deduces the following general idea from the consideration of these experiences:

"Superimposed upon self-consciousness as is that faculty upon simple-consciousness, a third and higher form of consciousness is at present making its appearance in our race. This higher form of consciousness, when it appears, occurs as it must, at the full maturity of the individual, at about the age of thirty-five, but almost always between the ages of thirty and forty. There have been occasional cases of it for the last two thousand years, and it is becoming more and more common. In fact, in all appearances, as far as observed, it obeys the laws to which every nascent faculty is subject. Many more or less perfect examples of this new faculty exist in the world today, and it has been my privilege to know personally and to have had the opportunity of studying, several men and women who have possessed it. In the course of a few more milleniums there should be born from the present human race, a higher type of man, possessing this higher type of consciousness. This new race, as it may well be called, would occupy toward us a position such as that occupied by us toward the simple conscious 'alulus homo.' The advent of this higher, better and happier race would simply justify the long agony of its birth through countless ages of our past. And it is the first article of my belief, some of the grounds for which I have endeavored to lay before you, that a new race is in course of evolution.''

In another part of his book, Dr. Bucke gives the following general characteristics of the special type of experiences recorded by him in the book:

''I have, in the last three years, collected twenty-three cases of this so-called cosmic consciousness. In each case the onset or incoming of the new faculty is always sudden, instantaneous. Among the unusual feelings the mind experiences is a sudden sense of being immersed in flame or in a brilliant light. This occurs entirely without worrying or outward cause, and may occur at noonday or in the middle of the night, and the person at first may feel that he is becoming insane. Along with these feelings comes a sense of immortality; not merely a feeling of certainty that there is a future life—that would be a small matter—but a pronounced **consciousness** that the life now being lived is eternal, death being seen as a trivial incident which does not affect its continuity. Further, there is an annihilation of the sense of sin, and an intellectual competency, not simply surpassing the old plane, but on an entirely new and higher plane. * * * The cosmic conscious race will not be the race that exists today, and more han the present is the same race that existed prior to the evolution of self-consciousness. A new race is being born from us, and this new race will in the near future possess the earth.''

Emerson is his wonderful essay on ''The Over-Soul'' clearly indicates his knowledge of the experiences mentioned herein in connection with what has been called ''Cosmic Consciousness.'' The following quotations therefrom will serve to disclose his general thought on the subject:

"Always, I believe, by the necessity of our constitution, a certain enthusiasm attends the individual's consciousness of that divine presence. The character and duration of this enthusiasm varies with the state of the individual, from an ecstasy and trance and prophetic inspiration—which is its rarer appearance —to the faintest glow of virtuous emotion, in which form it warms, like our household fires, all the families and associations of men, and makes society possible. A certain tendency to insanity has always attended the opening of the religious sense in men, as if 'blasted with excess of light.' The trances of Socrates; the 'Union' of Plotinus; the vision of Porphyry; the conversion of Paul; the aurora of Behmen; the convulsions of George Fox and his Quakers; the illumination of Swedenborg are of this kind. What was in the case of these remarkable persons a ravishment has in innumerable instances in common life been exhibited in a less striking manner. Everywhere the history of religion betrays a tendency to enthusiasm. The rapture of the Moravian and Quietist; the opening of the internal sense of the Word, in the language of the New Jerusalem Church; the revival of the Calvinistic Churches; the experiences of the Methodists, are varying forms of that shudder of awe and delight with which the individual soul always mingles with the universal soul. The nature of these revelations is always the same; they are perceptions of the absolute law. They are solutions of the soul's own questions. The soul answers never by words, but by the thing itself that is inquired after. * * * We live in succession, in division, in parts, in particles. Meantime within man is the soul of the whole; the wise silence; the universal beauty, to which every part and particle is equally related;

the eternal One. And this deep power in which we exist, and whose beatitude is all accessible to us, is not only self-sufficing and perfect in every hour, but the act of seeing, and the thing seen, the seer and the spectacle, the subject and the object, are One. We see the world piece by piece, as the sun and moon, the animal, the tree; but the whole, of which these are the shining parts, is the soul. It is only by the vision of that Wisdom that the horoscope of the ages can be read, and it is only by falling back on our better thoughts, by yielding to the spirit of prophesy which is innate in every man that we can know what it saith. Every man's words, who speaks from that life, must sound vain to those who do not dwell in the same thought on their own part. I dare not speak for it. My words do not carry its august sense; they fall short and cold. Only itself can inspire whom it will, and behold, their speech shall be lyrical and sweet, and universal as the rising of the wind. Yet I desire, even by profane words, if sacred I may not use, to indicate the heaven of this deity, and to report what hints I have collected of the transcendent simplicity and energy of the Highest Law.''

So such are the general reports of the nature and character of these glimpses of this Universal Consciousness which men here and there have experienced in all times. Let us now consider the **powers** kindled in those to whom glimpses (or more) of this consciousness has come. For an increase in ''knowing'' always brings with it an increase in power, according to the law of cause and effect.

In the first place, the possession by an individual of even a faint dawn of this Universal Consciousness, by whatever name it may be known, endows him with a certain "in touchness" with all the rest of Life. By a subtle intuition he may, under favorable circumstances, speak, write, paint, act, or produce music representing phase of vital, mental, and emotional activity transcending any actual experience on his own part. Such an individual becomes "en rapport" with, or "in tune" with, the manifold variety of living forms, and is able to produce a representation thereof through his own expression. This is the secret of the "genius" of great artists, writers, musicians, poets, and others who express through their own respective mediums or vehicles the messages they receive from the other forms of life with which they are connected by subtle filaments of unity. Such a one can "enter into" (in imagination) the life experiences of any and all forms of life, and to then represent them in visible or audible form in a degree depending upon their own development.

Moreover, such individuals are "universal" in their sympathies, and can feel with any form of life with which they come in contact. And as a consequence of the latter, they tend to inspire in other persons and living creatures a "liking," fellowship, and understanding. Many of the great illumined souls of the race, having this consciousness in at least some degree, find themselves "at home" with all manners and conditions of mankind, and in many cases with the lower life forms as well. Sympathy has been defined as "a fellow feeling," and it may be seen at once that when one has a feeling of fellowship with all Life (and such individuals have this to some degree), then there are created certain bonds and links of sympathy and unity which serve to unite the individual more or less strongly to all living things. In the case of the great teachers of the race, such as the founders of the great religions and similar souls, we find that universal sympathy with and understanding of all life which sets such individuals apart as marked and distinguished men, and imparts to them a universality which makes them citizens of all countries and dwellers in all time.

Again, we find that in the case of many individuals of this type there exists a certain power of attraction for other forms of life and things, which enables them to attract to themselves those conditions, environments, and persons best adapted to their wellbeing and happiness; and which also gives them certain so-called "miraculous" powers over Nature. He who is consciously identical with Nature is able to work "miracles" with Nature. We cannot go deeper into this subject at this time and place, for several very good reasons, but the above is a strong hint to those who are prepared to hear and understand the truth concerning certain phases of Life and Nature.

What we have said so far in our consideration of the individuals manifesting **flashes** or **glimpses** of this phase of consciousness, applies in a much greater degree to those who have **penetrated fully** into the higher sub-planes of this great Plane of Consciousness. On this planet, and on others, dwell Beings so fully awakened and unfolded in this phase of consciousness that they are as Supernatural Beings to the ordinary human being. Many of such beings are performing important offices in the unfoldment of the race, and the betterment of mankind. Many of these people have been regarded as Angels or Demi-Gods by ordinary people with whom they have come in contact in the past, and many of them are the Invisible Helpers of whose presence many of the race have been made aware by actual experiences.

Many of the White Magicians of the race belong to the higher phases of this great Plane of Consciousness. And, alas, some who are what is known as Black Magicians have managed to "break into the Kingdom of Heaven" on these planes, and have prostituted their power; but to such inevitably comes punishment by Nature herself, and are either forced into the legions of Light or else are disintegrated and destroyed by the very forces of Nature which they have set into operation for selfish and ignoble purposes.

VII. The Plane of the Consciousness of the Gods

If, as we have seen, it is most difficult to speak in understandable terms concerning the phases of life and activity on the last mentioned Plane of Consciousness, what must be the difficulty of even hinting at the life and activities of the highest plane of all—the Plane of the Consciousness of the Gods? On this highest of all Planes of Consciousness, however, dwell beings so high in the scale of knowledge, power, life, and bliss that even the imagination of the advanced student or teacher can scarcely grasp the idea. This is the Plane of the Gods, in verity—of being so far advanced that they are practically akin to the conception of the Gods created by man to account for the Universe, and to serve as objects of worship.

On this Plane are Personal Gods—many of them—but none of them, alone, may be regarded as GOD, in the sense of the Eternal Parent or Infinite Reality. For even the highest of them have their limitations and restrictions, and all are but Manifestations of the Infinite Unmanifest. Each of these exalted Beings has had its beginning or birth in Manifestation, and each will finally have its ending and disappearance into the Infinite Unmanifest, where all sense of separateness and personality will disappear.

The highest authorities inform us that the characteristic element of this highest form of all consciousness is the conscious realization of the individual that he IS identical with the Infinite, and is only **apparently** separated therefrom by the most tenuous and subtle veil of illusion.

Strange as it may appear to one not acquainted with the subject, glimpses and flashes of this consciousness, in rare instances, filter down into the consciousness of individuals on this earth at the present time, and have done so in the past. Many of the brave souls and keen minds of the Illumined have actually pierced the veil of this plane, and have been almost blinded by the light that has flashed upon them.

The consideration of this Plane of Consciousness must be closed here, for reasons which the advanced occultist will at once realize, and which the less advanced student must be told are adequate. Many, not prepared for the full Light must be protected from spiritual and mental blindness by being exposed to rays before they have become accustomed to the lesser lights of the Truth. Rest assured, however, O student, that when your eyes are ready to gaze upon the Sacred Flame, it will no longer be hidden from you.

The Truth in Symbols

There are certain truths which cannot be well expressed in words, but which may be at least partially expressed in symbols. To those who feel a desire to penetrate rather more deeply into the Mystery of the Three Higher Planes of Consciousness, we call attention to the symbol accompanying this particular chapter of this book. There is a wealth of knowledge and important information hidden in this symbol, undiscoverable to the many but at least partially discoverable by the few. To the Few, we offer the following suggestions concerning this Symbol.

Your attention is called to the fact that each circle in the symbol is called to and blended with the one on either side of it. Accordingly in the circular extent of each circle there is to be found FOUR different spaces or regions, as follows: (1) Its own unblended space or region; (2) the space or region in which its own space or region is blended with that of one of the neighboring circles, which constitutes a shield-shaped space; (3) the space or region in which its own space or region is blended with that of the other neighboring circle, constituting a shield-shaped space; and (4) the space or region in the very centre of the symbol, in which the space or region of each circle is blended with that of **both** of the other two—thus producing a Triune Region. This arrangement, again, furnishes us with SEVEN distinct regions, as follows (giving each circle the name of a letter, as A, B, or C, respectively) I. Circle A; II. Circle B; III. Circle C; IV. Space A-B; V. Space A-C; VI. Space B-C and finally VII. Region A-B-C, at the centre. There are thus three unblended areas; also three blended areas of two elements; and finally one blended area of three elements; the latter combining within itself all three elements in equal proportion. Let him who wishes for the Light solve this Riddle of the Symbol!

PART IX

THE SEVENFOLD SOUL OF MAN

In the Secret Doctrine of the Rosicrucians, we find the following Seventh Aphorism:

The Seventh Aphorism

VII. The Soul of Man is Sevenfold, yet but One in essence; Man's Spiritual Unfoldment has as its end the Discovery of Himself beneath the Sevenfold Veil.

In this Seventh Aphorism of Creation, the Rosicrucian is directed to apply his attention to the concept of the Sevenfold Soul—One in essence—of Man; which in the figurative language of the mystic constitutes the seven veils which conceal from (yet reveal to) Man his real Self. This concept is represented by the Rosicrucians by means of the symbol of the figure of a man surrounded by seven outlined shapes—the man, himself in his essence, is represented by the blank space disclosed by the inmost outline, and each one of the "concealing but revealing veils" is represented by an outlined figure, each being but one of the series of seven. The series of outlines, be it noted, is enclosed in the circle representing the Infinite Unmanifest.

The Symbol is interpreted as follows: (1) The Infinite Unmanifest manifests itself in the Elemental Soul; (2) the Elemental Soul takes upon itself the outward form of Mineral Substance; (3) The Mineral

Soul evolves from itself the Plant Soul; (4) the Plant
Soul evolves from itself the Animal Soul; (5) the
Animal Soul evolves from itself the Human Soul;
(6) the Human Soul unfolds into the Soul of the
Demi-Gods; (7) the Soul of the Demi-Gods unfolds
into the Soul of the Gods; and finally, the Soul of the
Gods once more is resolved into Pure Spirit, which

Figure 12. Symbol of the Sevenfold Soul

is represented by the blank space at the centre of
the symbol.   This statement will be more clearly
apprehended by those who have carefully studied the
preceding chapters conveying instruction concerning
the Seven Planes of Consciousness, and much of the
information contained in those chapters is to be
taken into consideration in the study of the present
chapter.

It will be noted that while these Seven Veils serve
to conceal the Real Self—in the sense of imposing

limitations and shape to it, yet at the same time it reveals the presence of Spirit by means of its outlines. The ancient teachers were wont to illustrate this concealing-revealment by means of a bit of thin gauzy drapery suspended across the space of an open door or open window into which the breeze is blowing. The drapery covers (and thus conceals) the moving wind, yet at the same time it shows a form representing the movement and presence of the wind, and thus reveals the latter. Another favorite illustration was that of an invisible hand, of itself impossible of being perceived, but upon which was placed seven gloves, one over the other. The gloves were filled, and the presence of the hand revealed; but each glove, in turn, is mistaken for the hand itself. The hand is able to feel but faintly, and to act clumsily when the gloves are all on it, but as each glove is taken off it feels more sensitively, and performs more delicate actions; but without at least one of the gloves it is not apparent at all, even to the eyes of its owner.

Let us now briefly consider each of these Veils with which Spirit is concealed, and yet revealed.

I. The Elemental Soul

There is only one REAL Soul, of course; and when the Rosicrucians speak of "The Elemental Soul" they mean simply the Soul clad in the garments of elemental substance—covered with the veil of elemental substance, which while concealing its real nature yet serves to reveal it in manifestation.

Following the terms of the symbol, it may be said that the Infinite Unmanifest involves itself first in the garment of Elemental Substance, or wraps itself in the veil thereof. Elemental Substance, in the sense in which the term is used by the Rosicrucians in this connection, is a very subtle, tenuous form of substance—a form of substance which may be regarded as the "ancestor" of the most subtle form of matter known to science today. It lies far back of the plane of the electrons, ions, or corpuscles of which matter (as commonly known) is composed.

The Elemental Soul, clad in the garments of Elemental Matter is the **pattern** upon which the ordinary physical body is built. It is the "ghost" of the physical body, and persists after the disintegration of the latter. The **intelligence** or **consciousness** manifesting in this garment of substance is quite simple and elementary, and performs merely the office of providing and sustaining a **pattern** or **form** upon which the ordinary physical body is built.

This Elemental Soul, embodied in elemental substance as stated, is that Something which to the race has been known as the "ghost," "spirit" (in this case the term "spirit" is grossly misused and inappropriate), ethereal body, "fluidic body," "double," "wraith," "doppelganger," etc. It has sometimes been called "the astral body," but this is a mistake, for what the occultists have long known as the true "astral body" is something very different.

This Elementary Soul survives the dissolution of the physical body of the individual to which it belonged, and under certain conditions and circumstances it may become visible to living persons as the "ghost" of the deceased person. When the Elementary Soul has been "sloughed off" by the higher vehicles of the Soul (after the physical "death"), and has also been released by the partial or complete disintegration of the physical body, it is really but a "shell" having for form and shape of the latter, and is almost lifeless, although held together by the cohesive forces of the fast-dying vibrations. In such cases it possesses neither intelligence nor consciousness beyond that concerned in holding its substance together and to all intents and purposes can be regarded as nothing more than a **mass of cloudy vapor assuming the form of a human being**, and destined to become speedily disintegrated on its own plane.

II. The Mineral Soul

By the term "The Mineral Soul," the Rosicrucians seek to indicate the Soul embodied in the Mineral or Chemical Substance of which the Physical Body is composed. The concept sought to be expressed is the physical body of man considered merely in its aspect of mineral or chemical substance and their atoms—rather than in its aspect of protoplasmatic, **living** substance (using the term "living" in its popular, rather than in its esoteric sense).

The term "Mineral" of course means "inorganic substances having a definite chemical composition; neither animal nor vegetable substances." We need scarcely to call the attention of the student to the fact that the substance of which the physical body is composed is, itself, composed of certain chemical or mineral substances, such as oxygen, carbon, hydrogen, nitrogen, sulphur, phosphorus, iron, and other chemical elements. Cremate a body and the greater part of it will disappear as the vapor of water (composed of oxygen and hydrogen), and other gases; the remainder being composed of other chemical or mineral elements. The physical body is built up of mineral and chemical elements transformed by the action of plant chemistry into protoplasm, and then absorbed by man as food in the form of vegetables or animal meat. The basis of all organic matter is chemical or mineral substance. Protoplasm, the basis of organic substance, vegetable or animal, was evolved from carbon—that same element which manifests as coal, diamond, graphite, etc. The physical basis of the bodies of animals and plants is solely mineral or chemical, and all such bodies are built up from the chemical material originally furnished by earth, air, and water.

The intelligence and consciousness manifested in and by the Mineral Soul is confined to that required for the purely chemical processes of the body, and the coordination and regulation of the chemical and mineral particles of which the body is composed. There are important chemical processes under way in the life of the physical body—many of them quite complicated, so complicated in fact that they cannot be reproduced or duplicated in the laboratory of man's making and operation. These important processes are under the control and direction of the Mineral Soul—of Soul embodied in the chemical and mineral substance of which the body is composed. These processes are not merely mechanical—they are the product of intelligence and consciousness, and are impossible without the presence of these mental forces.

When the physical body is discarded by the soul at "death," it proceeds to disintegrate; first the organic substances of which it is composed, i. e., the vegetable and animal organic material, become resolved into their mineral and chemical elements, and then these, in turn, become resolved into their more simple forms and conditions, and are used in supplying material for the bodies of other forms of living creatures.

III. The Plant Soul

By the term "The Plant Soul," the Rosicrucians seek to indicate the Soul embodied in the Vegetable Cellular Substance of which a very large proportion of the human physical body is composed. Apart from advanced scientists and advanced occultists, few realize how great proportion of the processes of the human and animal body is really vegetable in nature. The growth of bodily tissue, of parts and organs, is distinctively vegetable in character.

Recent discoveries in the biological laboratories and in the realms of surgery have shown us that not only portions of skin and bone may be "grafted" from one body to another, and made to grow as well in the new body as in the old; not only that portions of organs may be "transplanted" in a similar way and made to grow and perform their offices; but also that portions of the human body, and organs thereof, may be removed from the original body, and made to grow and perform their offices independent of the bodily general organism. And these processes are not merely chemical—they manifest all the characteristics of purely vegetable processes.

The chief distinction between the intelligence and consciousness of Plants and Animals is that the former manifest almost entirely along the lines of instinctive or unconscious mentation, while the latter manifest in a steadily increasing degree purpositive and deliberate conscious activity. In the processes of the human body we find a large proportion of those performed clearly along the lines of the instinctive, unconscious vegetable kingdom. These processes come under the control and direction of the Plant Soul. They are performed on the Plane of Plant Consciousness just as truly as are the processes of the ordinary types of plant life. Some of these processes are very complex—but so are the processes involved in the life of the ordinary plant.

The distinction between the plane of the Plant Soul and that of the Animal Soul will become more apparent and clear as we proceed to consider the phenomena of the latter.

IV. The Animal Soul

By the term "The Animal Soul," the Rosicrucians seek to indicate the Soul embodied in the Animal Organic Substance, both in the lower animals and in man. The Animal Soul is the animating spirit, or vital spirit, manifesting in the many activities of animal life, high and low. Its intelligence and consciousness are very high in comparison to those of the Vegetable Soul, but is limited to the requirements and needs of the purely animal life. In its lower manifestations it is but little if any higher than that of the higher manifestations of the Plant Life, and in its highest manifestations it is but little if any lower than that of the lowest manifestations of the Human Soul. In fact, as we have repeatedly said in this book, the various Planes of Consciousness (and hence the powers and limits of the several Souls) blend into those on each side of them, and with which they are linked.

The Animal Soul is the seat of the purely animal desires, and in the work of developing and satisfying the same it has built up out of the substance of which it is composed, and which it has absorbed from the substances of the vegetable and mineral plane beneath it, certain complex organs and groups of organs. Its intelligence and consciousness are concerned simply with the **physical well-being** of their owner, the man, just as in the animal they are concerned with the physical well-being of the animal owner. Moreover, certain of the purely vegetable processes, such as nutrition, reproduction, etc., are in part taken over by the Animal Soul and additional power and complexity bestowed upon them. The desires of man which we usually refer to as ''purely physical'' belong to the Animal Soul. The chief desires of the Animal Soul are concerned with the offices of nutrition and reproduction, and manifest respectively as Self Preservation and Sex Desire (on the physical plane, of course), and as Love of Offspring.

In its higher phases the Animal Soul develops and manifests certain higher qualities, such as the desire for Comradeship, Companionship, Mutual Sympathy, Affection, etc., which closely resembles similar feelings and emotions in the lower animals—this because the two Planes of Consciousness are linked together and are blended one with the other. The Animal Soul, however, never has the consciousness of ''I Am''—at the most it may be conscious as ''Am,'' but the ''I'' consciousness is never present in its true form.

V.   The Human Soul

The Human Soul is distinguished from the Animal Soul not only by its special aptitude for intellectual reasoning, and voluntary choice and action, but also by its consciousness of itself—of the ''I am I.'' This distinction has been fully explained in previous chapters of this book, and need not be gone into in further detail at this place. The following paragraph, however, quoted from a writer, may prove of interest in the consideration of this phase of the general subject before us. The writer says:

"Among the lower animals there is very little of what may be called Self Consciousness. In fact, the consciousness of the lowest forms of animal life is little more than mere sensation. Life in the early stages of animal life is almost automatic. The mentation there is almost entirely along subconscious lines, and the mental operations are only those which are concerned with the physical life of the animal—the satisfaction of its primitive wants. After a bit, this primitive consciousness developed into what psychologists call 'simple consciousness,' which is an 'awareness' of outside things, and an apprehension of them as 'things.' But there is no self-consciousness manifested at this point. The animal does not think of its hopes and fears, its aspirations, its plans, its thoughts, and then compare them with like thoughts of others of its kind. It cannot indulge in abstract thinking, or use symbols of thought. It simply takes things for granted and asks no questions. It does not seek to find answers to perplexing general questions, for it does not know that such questions exist. With the advent of Self-Consciousness, man begins to form a conception of the 'I'. He begins to compare himself with others, and to reason about the result thereof. He takes mental stock of himself, and draws conclusions from what he finds in his mind. He begins to think for himself, to analyze, to classify, to separate, to deduce, to form judgments. He begins to create for himself, and is no longer a mere mental automaton."

Another writer has said concerning the evolution

of the consciousness of man: "For some hundreds of years, upon the general plane of self-consciousness, an ascent, to the human eye gradually, but from the point of view of cosmic evolution rapid, has been made. In a race, large-brained, walking erect, gregarious, brutal, but king of all other brutes, man in appearance but not in fact, was from the highest simple consciousness born the basic human faculty, Self Consciousness, and its twin, Language. From these and what went with these, through suffering, toil, and war; through bestiality, savagery, barbarism; through slavery, greed, effort; through conquest infinite, through defeats overwhelming, through struggle unending; through ages of aimless semi-brutal existence; through subsistence on berries and roots; through the use of the casually found stone or stick; through life in deep forests, with nuts and seeds, and on the shores of waters, with mollusks, crustaceans, and fish for food; through that greatest, perhaps, of human victories, the domestication and subjugation of fire; through the invention and art of bow and arrow; through the taming of animals and the breaking of them to labor; through the long learning which led to the cultivation of the soil; through the abode brick and the building of houses therefrom; through the smelting of metals and the slow birth of the arts which rest upon these; through the slow making of alphabets and the evolution of the written word; in short, through thousands of centuries of human life, of human aspiration, of human growth, sprang the world of men and women as it stands before us and within us today with all its achievements and possessions."

A writer on the subject of the evolution of the soul has well given the following words of warning: "The awakening of the intellect in man does not necessarily make him a better being. While it is true that the unfolding of a higher faculty gives an upward tendency to man, it is also true that some men are so closely wrapped in the folds of the animal sheath— so steeped in the material side of things—that the awakened intellect only tends to give them increased powers to gratify their low desires and inclinations. Man, if he chooses, may excel the beasts in bestiality —he may descend to depths of which the beast never would have thought. The beast is governed solely by instinct, and his actions, so prompted, are perfectly natural and proper, and the animal is not to be blamed for following the impulses of his nature. But man, in whom intellect has unfolded, knows that it is contrary to his highest nature to descend to the level of the beasts—yea, lower by far. He adds to the brute desires the cunning and intelligence which have come to him, and deliberately prostitutes his higher principle to the task of carrying out the magnified animal propensities. Very few animals abuse their desires—it is left for some men to do so. The higher the degree of intellect unfolded in a man, the greater the depths of low passions, appetites, and desires possible to him. He may actually create new brute desires, or rather, build edifices of his own upon the brute foundations. It is unnecessary for us to state that all occultists know that such a course will bring certain consequences in its train, which will result in the soul having to spend many weary years in retracing its steps over the backward road it has trodden. Its progress has been retarded, and it will be compelled to retravel the road to freedom, in common with the beastlike natures of undeveloped creatures whose proper state of the journey it is, having an additional burden in the shape of the horror of a consciousness of its surroundings, whereas its beast-companions have no such consciousness and suffer not therefrom. If you can imagine the feeling of a cultured, civilized man being compelled to dwell among the African Bushmen for many years, with a full recollection of his past living in civilization, you may form a faint idea of the fate in store for one who deliberately sinks his higher powers to the accomplishment of low ends and desires. But even for such a soul there is escape—in time."

The Human Soul occupies a place of great trials and struggles between two conflicting forces. On the one hand is the force of the lower animal nature, striving to pull it downward into the plane of the Animal Soul and urging him to employ his newly awakened intellectual powers on the lower plane. On the other hand is the awakening forces of the higher spiritual nature, striving to draw him upward into a consciousness of his relationship to the All, and urging him to open his intellect to the inflow of the higher vibrations of spiritual consciousness and to turn his faculties to the carrying out of the dictates of the higher portion of himself.

VI.   The Soul of the Demi-Gods

As has been said in the preceding chapters of this book, the Soul of the Demi-Gods has as its distinctive and characteristic consciousness the conscious realization of its relationship to the All—to the Universal Life. Its mental and spiritual horizon has expanded until, in its higher stages, it takes in All Life and feels itself identified therewith. All that has come to man of humanity, justice, kindness, sympathy, nobility and Human Brotherhood has come to him filtered through from this higher region of himself. Man feels sympathy for others because of his dawning sense of his relationship to, or Oneness with all the rest. With the coming of the flashes of the Cosmic Consciousness, all narrow feelings of distinction and caste fade away, and he feels the urge of Unity. Not only does he enjoy the thrill of Universal Life, but he also may suffer the World-Pain, at least until a fuller understanding of the latter comes to him.

A writer has well said of this stage of consciousness: "As man unfolds spiritually, he feels his relationship with all mankind, and he begins to love his fellow-man more and more. It hurts him to see others suffering, and when it hurts him enough he tries to do something to remedy it. As time goes on and man develops, the terrible suffering which many human beings undergo today will be impossible, for the reason that the unfolding spiritual consciousness of the race will make the pain be felt so severely by all that the race will not be able to stand it any longer, and it will rebel and insist that matters be remedied. From the inner recesses of the soul comes a protest against the following of the lower animal nature, and, although we may put it aside for a time, it will become more and more persistent, until finally we will be forced to heed it. The struggle between the higher and lower natures has been noticed by all careful observers of the human soul, and many theories have been advanced to account for it. In former times it was taught that man was being tempted by the devil on the one hand, and helped by a guardian angel on the other hand. But, as all occultists know, the struggle is between the two elements of man's nature, not exactly warring, but each following its own line of effort, and the Ego is torn and bruised in its efforts to adjust itself. The Ego is in a transition stage of consciousness, and the struggle is quite painful at times, but the growing soul in time rises above the attraction of the lower nature, and its dawning spiritual consciousness enables to understand his real nature and his real place in the universe.''

The same writer has said: ''The higher planes of the soul are also the source of the 'inspiration' which certain poets, painters, sculptors, writers, preachers, orators, and others have received in all times and in all lands. This is the source from which the seer obtains his vision—the prophet his insight and foresight. Many have concentrated themselves upon high ideals in their work, and have received rare knowledge from this source, attributing it to beings of another world—but the inspiration came from within: it was the voice of the Higher Self speaking to the Ego.''

The writer aforesaid, informs us as follows concerning the experiences of Inspiration and Illumination coming to the Ego from the regions of this Higher Self: ''These experiences, of course, vary materially according to the degree of unfoldment of the individual, his previous training, his temperament, etc., but there are certain characteristics common to all. The common features are as follows: (1) A conviction of a sense of actual being—of immortality; this apart from faith or religious conviction, and coming seemingly from a deeper source than these—it has been described as 'the faith that knows.' (2) A total slipping away of all fear and the acquirement of a feeling of trust, certainty, and confidence, which is beyond the comprehension of those who have never experienced it. (3) A feeling of universal Love which sweeps over one—a Love which includes all Life, from those near to one in the flesh to those at the furthest parts of the universe; from those whom we hold as pure and holy, to those whom we have regarded as vile, wicked, and utterly unworthy. All feelings of self-righteousness and condemnation seem to slip away, and one's love, like the light of the sun, falls upon all alike, irrespective of their degree of development or 'goodness.' (4) A feeling of the utmost bliss and joy, the memory of which abides long after the actual experience. (5) A feeling of exalted knowledge and wisdom, in which all doubt disappears and a sense of understanding the deeper meaning of all things takes its place, for the time of the experience at least. To some these experiences have come as a deep reverent mood or feeling, which took possession of them for a time, while others have seemed to be in a dream and have become conscious of a spiritual uplifting accompanied by a sensation of being surrounded by a brilliant and all-pervading light or glow. To some, certain truths have become manifest in the form of symbols, the full meaning of which in some cases have not become apparent until long after the actual experience.

"These experiences, when they have come to one, have left him in a new state of mind, and he has never been the same man afterward. Although the keenness of the recollection has worn off, there remains a certain memory which long afterward proves a source of comfort and strength to him, especially when he feels faint of faith and is shaken like a reed by the winds of conflicting opinions and speculations. The memory of such an experience is a source of renewed strength—a haven of refuge to which the weary soul flies for shelter from the outside world which understands it not. From the writings of the ancient philosophers of all races, from the songs of the great poets of all peoples, from the preachings of the prophets of all religions and times we can gather traces of this illumination which has come to them—this unfoldment of spiritual consciousness. One tells the story in one way, the other in other terms, but all tell practically the same essential story. All who have recognized this illumination, even in a faint degree, recognize the like experience in the tale, song, or preaching of another, though centuries may roll between them. It is the song of the Soul, which when once heard is never forgotten. Though it be sounded by the crude instruments of the semi-barbarous races, or the finished instruments of the talented musician of today, its strains are plainly recognized. From Old Egypt comes the song—from India of all ages—from Ancient Greece and Rome—from the early Christian saint—from the Quaker Friend—from the Catholic monastaries—from the Mohammedan Mosque—from the Chinese Philosopher—from the legends of the American Indian hero-prophet—it is always the same strain, and it is swelling louder and louder, as many more are taking it up and adding their voices or the sounds of their instruments to the grand chorus.''

The student must remember that in the experiences noted above, the individual simply has flashes, or period of dawning consciousness on this Sixth Plane of Consciousness, and is not to be regarded as having entered fully and completely into its manifestations, much less as having evolved into a state in which he functions normally and habitually on this high plane. There are beings—once men—who have evolved into the higher state in which they function normally and habitually on this plane of conscious being; but these individuals are no more than mere men, and have earned the right to be called "Demi-Gods." But, even as they once were men, so all men become as they now are by the unfoldment of this higher region of Self. These flashes of consciousness from this high plane are prophetic signs and messages indicating the awakening of the higher faculties, and giving assurance of further growth and unfoldment.

In concluding our consideration of this high plane, let us glance at the following words from the pen of Sir Oliver Lodge, the great English scientist, who has given the world startling corroboration of some important ancient truths known to the occultists and esoteric teachers; he says: "Let us imagine, then, as a working hypothesis, that our subliminal self—the other and greater part of us—is in touch with another order of existence, and that it is occasionally able to communicate, or somehow, perhaps unconsciously, transmit to the fragment in the body something of the information accessible to it. We should then be like icebergs floating in an ocean, with only a fraction exposed to the sun and air and observation; the rest, by far the greater bulk, eleven-twelfths —submerged in a connecting medium, submerged and occasionally in subliminal or sub-aqueous contact with others, while still the peaks, the visible bergs, are far separate. Such an iceberg, glorying in its crisp solidity and sparkling pinnacles, might resent attention paid to its submerged subliminal supporting region, or to the saline liquid out of which it arose, and to which in due course it will some day return. 'We feel that we are greater than we know.' Or, reversing the metaphor, we might liken our present state to that of the hulls of ships submerged in a dim ocean among strange beasts, propelled in a blind manner through space; proud, perhaps, of accumulating many barnacles of decoration: only recognizing our destination by bumping against the dock wall; and with no cognizance of the deck, and the cabins, and spars, and sails, no thought of the sextant and the compass and the captain, no perception of the lookout on the mast, of the distant horizon, no vision of objects far ahead, dangers to be avoided, destinations to be reached, other ships to be spoken with by means other than by bodily contact—a region of sunshine and cloud, of space, of perception, and of intelligence, utterly inaccessible to those parts below the water line.''

VII. The Soul of the Gods

It must be apparent to every careful student that it is practically impossible to speak in ordinary terms of the expression and manifestation of the Self which is known to the Rosicrucians as ''The Soul of the Gods.'' It is sufficient for the purpose to merely indicate its existence as a phase of the Ego—existing in a latent state in most individuals, but affording occasional flashes of its presence to a few, and destined to become the normal plane of conscious functioning to the whole race in the course of spiritual evolution. Moreover, on certain planes of life and being, even today, there exist beings to whom this phase of consciousness is habitual and normal, even as is the plane of human consciousness normal and habitual to the majority of our race today.

To such beings, separated from the Infinite Unmanifest—the Eternal Parent—but by the most tenuous and subtle substance serving as the veil, the whole process of the Universe must appear merely as a great moving picture show of shadow forms, magnificent phantasmagoria having apparent substance and form but having no actual reality when viewed from the aspect of the Eternal. Such beings are, indeed, Gods as compared with the rest of living creatures. Close up to the very heart of the Eternal, these exalted beings are conscious of the very heart-throbs of the Eternal Parent.

As almost incredible as it may seem, however, there are among us on earth today certain advanced souls in whom this consciousness has already begun to manifest itself; and their number is growing. Such souls have experienced an actual conscious realization of the truth that the One is All, and that other than the One there is nothing—the entire array of the Cosmic Phantasmagoria being perceived as Illusion, Mirage, Maya, Glamour, Unreality. Into such, the Soul of the Gods is beginning to manifest itself.

No more can be said here on this particular subject.

Summary

The student must not fall into the error of supposing that man really has seven separate and distinct souls, either tied together like a bundle of twigs, or else worn as one would wear seven overcoats, one over the other. The symbol is only figurative, and must not be construed literally. There are not seven selves in man—but only One Self concealed by seven veils, each of which while serving to conceal the real nature of the Self yet serves to disclose the presence and power thereof to some degree. It is as if seven planes of variously colored glass, ranging from the darkest to the almost-transparent and colorless, were to be placed before a brilliant light. The darker glass would almost entirely obscure the Light, though yet revealing its presence in some of its rays; the next lighter would reveal more, and obscure less; and so on to the last in which the obscuration was but slight, and the revelation almost perfect. All illustrations of this ineffable fact of the Eternal are, by the very nature of things, imperfect, faulty, and misleading if taken too literally.

The lesson to the student is that in every man there lie concealed the potentiality of Godhood, and stages less than Godhood though above that of ordinary Manhood; and that in every man also abide the lower phases of manifested existence, even the very lowest of all. The wise man uses the lower, but does not allow the lower to use him; he maintains a positive, masterful mental attitude toward the lower planes of being, while opening himself receptively to the influences of the higher planes of his Self.

In conclusion, you are asked to once more consider the Seventh Aphorism: "The Soul of Man is Sevenfold, yet but One in essence: Man's spiritual Unfoldment has as its end the Discovery of Himself beneath the Seven-fold Veil."

PART X

METEMPSYCHOSIS

The Rosicrucians hold as a very important part of the teaching the occult doctrine of Metempsychosis, Reincarnation, or Transmigration of Souls, the essence of which doctrine is the survival of the individual soul after it passes from the physical body in death, and its reembodiment in a physical body by rebirth after a sojourn in the resting place of the souls.

The doctrine of Metempsychosis is one of the oldest of the human race. Traces of the teaching are found in the records of practically every one of the ancient races in all parts of the globe. In one form or another it has existed in the esoteric circles to be found at the heart of each of the world's great religions, including Christianity. It has always been a cardinal doctrine in the religions of the Orient, and during the past twenty-five years has attained a wonderful revival of popularity among the thinkers of the Occident.

The Rosicrucians' teachings hold that the Evolution of Man has been accomplished not alone by the general evolutionary trend of the race by which it moves forward from generation to generation, but also by the advance and ascent caused by the improvement in the reincarnating individual soul, each step of rebirth tending upward and onward. As a writer has said: ''The teachings hold that Evolution is caused by the soul striving, struggling, and pressing forward toward fuller and still fuller expression, using Matter as a material, and yet always struggling to free itself from the confining and retarding influence of the latter.   The struggle results in an unfoldment, causing sheath after sheath of the confining material bonds to be thrown off and discarded, as the spirit moulds matter to serve its higher purposes.   Evolution is but the process of birth of the imprisoned spirit, unfolding and extricating itself from the web of matter in which it has been involved and infolded.   And the pains and struggles are but incidents of the spiritual parturition.''

The Rosicrucians have no special, distinctive theories concerning Metempsychosis, but, on the contrary, accept the general teaching of the ancient occultists concerning reembodiment of the soul. They regard re-birth as just as natural as birth, and consider that the race has at its disposal a vast volume of actual experiences of individuals which conclusively proves the truth of the doctrine.   In fact, the Rosicrucian teachers make no attempt to **argue** the question with the student; but, rather, present the teaching as it comes to them, backed up by the wealth of authority on the part of the ancient schools, and fortified by the innumerable personal recollections on the part of individuals—in most cases the student himself has an intuition of the truth of the doctrine, in the first place, and often has a greater or less degree of recollection of his former lives on earth.

Metempsychosis has always been the accepted belief of many of the most intelligent members of the race.   It is found to have been the inner doctrine of the ancient Egyptians, and was held in the highest regard by the great thinkers of the ancient Western world, such as Pythagoras, Empedocles, Plato, Virgil, and Ovid. Plato's teachings were filled with the doctrine. Ths Hindu philosophies are based upon it. The Persian Magi held implicitly to it. The ancient Druids, and the Priests of Gaul taught it. Traces of the doctrine are found in the records of the ancient races of the Aztecs, the Peruvians, and other old peoples of the New World. The Eleusinian Mysteries of Greece, the Roman Mysteries of the Temple, the Inner Doctrines of the Kabbala of the Hebrews, all were based upon the doctrine of Metempsychosis. The early Christian Fathers, the Gnostics and Manichaens and other early Christian sects, believed in it. The great philosophers, ancient and modern, treated it with respect if indeed they did not fully accept it in many cases. The following quotations from modern authorities give an idea of the importance attached to the doctrine by modern thinkers:

Hedge says: "Of all the theories respecting the origin of the soul, Metempsychosis seems to me the most plausible and therefore the one most likely to throw light on the question of the life to come." James Freeman Clarke says: "It would be curious if we would find science and philosophy taking up again the old theory of metempsychosis, remodeling it to suit our present modes of religious and scientific thought, and launching it again on the wide ocean of human belief. But stranger things have happened in the history of human opinions." Professor Knight says: "If we could legitimately determine any question of belief by the number of its adherents, the decision would be in favor of metempsychosis rather than to any other.   I think it is quite as likely to be revived and to come to the front as any rival theory.''   Professor Bowen says: ''It seems to me, a firm and well-grounded faith in the doctrine of Christian metempsychosis might help to regenerate the world.   For it would be a faith not hedged around with many of the difficulties and objections which beset other forms of doctrines, and it offers distinct and pungent motives for trying to lead a more Christian life, and for loving and helping our brother man.   The doctrine of Metempsychosis may almost claim to be a natural or innate belief in the human mind, if we may judge from its wide diffusion among the nations of the earth, and its prevalence throughout the historical ages.''   E. D. Walker says: ''When Christianity first swept over Europe, the inner thought of its leaders was deeply tinctured with this truth.   The Church tried effectually to eradicate it, but in various sects it kept sprouting forth beyond the time of Erigina and Bonaventura, its mediaeval advocates.   Every great intuitional soul, as Paracelsus, Boehme, and Swedenborg, has adhered to it.   The Italian luminaries, Giordano Bruno and Campanella, embraced it.   The best of German philosophy is enriched by it.   In Schopenhauer, Lessing, and Fichte the younger, it is earnestly advocated.   The anthropological systems of Kant and Schelling furnish points of contact with it.   The younger Helmont adduces in two hundred problems all the arguments which may be urged in favor of the return of souls into human bodies, according to Jewish ideas.   Of English thinkers, the Cambridge Platonists defended it with much learning and acuteness, most conspicuously Henry More; and in Cudsworth and Hume it ranks as the most rational theory of immortality. Glanvil devotes a curious treatise to it. It captivated the minds of Fourier and Leroux. Andre Pezzani's book on the Plurality of the Soul's Lives works out the system on the Roman Catholic idea of expiation.''

But, better than all the opinions and shades of belief found among the great writers and teachers concerning this important subject, is the inner conviction of all souls which have reached a certain stage of spiritual unfoldment—the conviction that ''I have lived before.'' Such a conviction and intuitive belief based upon the reawakening of dim memories, is worth more to an individual than tons of printed opinions on the subject.

A writer has said on this point: ''Who has not experienced the consciousness of having felt the thing before—of having thought it at some time in the dim past? Who has not witnessed new scenes that appear old, very old? Who has not met persons for the first time, whose presence has awakened memories of a past lying far back in the misty ages of long ago? Who has not been seized at times with the consciousness of a mighty 'oldness' of soul? Who has not heard music, often entirely new compositions, which somehow awakened memories of similar strains, scenes, places, faces, voices, lands, associations and events, sounding dimly on the strings of memory as the breezes of the harmony float over them? Who has not gazed at some old painting, or piece of statuary, with the sense of having seen it all before? Who has not lived through events which brought with them a certainty of their being merely a repetition of some shadowy occurrences away back in lives lived long ago? Who has not felt the influence of the mountain, the sea, the desert, coming to them when they are far away from such scenes—coming so vividly as to cause the actual scene of the present to fade into comparative unreality? Who has not had these experiences?''

Sir Walter Scott once made the following observation in his diary: ''I cannot, I am sure, tell if it is worth marking down, that yesterday, at dinner time, I was strangely haunted by what I would call the sense of preexistence, viz.: a confused idea that nothing that passed was said for the first time; that the same topics had been discussed and the same persons had stated the same opinions on them. The sensation was so strong as to resemble what is called a mirage in the desert, and a calenture on board ship. * * * Why is it that some scenes awaken thoughts which belong as it were to dreams of early and shadowy recollections, such as the old Brahmins would have ascribed to a state of previous existence? How often do we find ourselves in society which we have never before met, and yet feel impressed with a mysterious and ill-defined consciousness that neither the scene nor the speakers nor the subject are entirely new; nay, feel as if we could anticipate that part of the conversation which has not yet taken place.''

Bulwer says: ''There is a strange kind of inner and spiritual memory which so often recalls to us places and persons we have never seen before, and which Platonists would resolve to be the unquenched consciousness of a former life. How strange is it that at times a feeling comes over us as we gaze upon certain places, which associates the scene either with some dim remembered and dreamlike images of the Past, or with a prophetic and fearful omen of the Future. Everyone has known a similar strange and indistinct feeling at certain times and places, and with a similar inability to trace the cause." Poe says: "We walk about, amid the destinies of our world existence, accompanied by dim but ever present memories of a Destiny more vast— very distant in the by-gone time and infinitely awful. We live out a youth peculiarly haunted by such dreams, yet never mistaking them for dreams. As memories we know them. During our youth the distinctness is too clear to deceive us even for a moment; but the doubt of manhood dispels them as illusions." Charles Dickens once wrote: "In the foreground was a group of silent peasant girls, leaning upon the parapet of the little bridge, looking now up at the sky, now down at the water; in the distance a deep dell; the shadow of an approaching night on everything. If I had been murdered there in some former life I could not have seemed to remember the place more thoroughly, or with more emphatic chilling of the blood; and the real remembrance of it acquired in that minute is so strengthened by the imaginary recollection that I hardly think I could forget it."

If evidence of the truth of Metempsychosis other than personal intuition and glimpses of memory of past lives were needed, we would find such evidence in the phenomena of the infant prodigies, and cases of childhood genius, instance of which abound on all sides. Children at a very early age manifest evidences of a deep knowledge of mathematics, music, art, etc., even in cases where the explanation of heredity fails to fit the case. The case of Mozart gives us a typical case of this kind. The child, Mozart, at the age of four was able not only to perform difficult pieces of music on the piano, but also to compose original works of merit. Not only did he manifest the highest faculty of sound and note, but also an instinctive ability to compose and arrange music, which ability was far superior to that of many men who had devoted years of their life to the study and practice of music. The laws of harmony, the science of commingling tones, was to this wonderful child not the work of years, but a faculty born in him.

Another marked case is that of Zerah Colburn, the mathematical prodigy, whose feats attracted the attention of the scientific world during the last century. In this case, the child under eight years of age, without any previous knowledge of even the common rules of arithmetic, or even of the use and powers of the Arabic numerals, solved a great variety of arithmetical problems by a simple operation of the mind, and without the use of any visible symbols or contrivances. He could answer readily a question involving the statement of the exact number of minutes or seconds in any given period of time. He could also state with equal facility the exact product of the multiplication of any number containing two, three, or four figures by another number consisting of a like number of figures. He could state almost instantly all the factors composing a number of six or seven places of figures. He could likewise determine instantly questions concerning the extraction of the square and cube roots of any number proposed, and likewise whether it was a prime number incapable of division by any other number, for which there is no known general rule among mathematicians. Asked such questions in the midst of his ordinary childish play, he would answer them almost instantly and then proceed with his play.

This child once undertook and completely succeeded in raising the number 8 progressively up to the sixteenth power—in naming the result, 281,474,-976, 710, 656 he was absolutely correct in every figure. He could raise any given number progressively up to the 10th power, with so much speed that the person putting down the figures on paper would frequently request him to manifest less speed. He gave instantly the square root of 106,929, and the cube root of 268,336,125. He could give the prime factors of very large numbers, and could detect large prime numbers instantly. Once asked how many minutes there were in forty-eight years, and before the question could be written down he answered "25,228,800", adding "and the number of seconds in such period is 1,513,728,000." The child, when questioned concerning his ability to give such answers, and to solve such difficult problems, was unable to give such information. He could say that he did not know how the answer came into his mind, but it was evident from watching him that some actual process was under way in his mind, and that there was no question of mere trick of memory in his feats. Moreover, it is important to note that he was totally ignorant of even the common rules of arithmetic, and could not "figure" on slate or paper even the simplest sum in addition or multiplication. It is interesting to note the sequel to this case, i. e., the fact that when a few years later the child was sent to the common schools and was there instructed in the art of written arithmetic, his power began to vanish, and eventually it left him altogether, and he became no more than any other child of his age. It seemed as if some door of his soul had been closed, while before it had stood ajar.

The Rosicrucians teach that the human soul is on the path of progress, learning the lessons of life and experience, life after life, and storing away the essence of these impressions which go to form the basis of the "character" of the individual when he is reborn. The rebirth, or the conditions thereof, are not forced upon the individual soul, according to the Rosicrucian teachings, but, on the contrary the individual soul is attracted toward rebirth by reason of the presence of certain desires in its character—or rather, by reason of the essence of its desires. It is reborn into certain environments solely because it has within itself certain unsatisfied desires which could be satisfied only in just those environments. The operation of the Law of Attraction is justly regular here as in the attraction of the atoms of matter.

Each soul contains within itself the attracting force of certain sets of desires, and this force attracts to the soul certain conditions and experiences and also attracts such experiences and conditions to the soul. There is no element of punishment, or of injustice, in the operation of this law, for it gives to each soul just what the soul requires to meet its indwelling unsatisfied desires, or else the conditions and experiences which will serve to burn out of the soul certain desires which are holding it back in its progress, the destruction of which will make possible future advancement.

The Rosicrucians teach that the individuals of any sub-race who have outstripped their fellows in spiritual unfoldment, are still bound by race ties to their brothers left behind—that is, up to a certain point. In many cases such individuals are compelled until the great body of the sub-race moves up to the position of the individual. But such individuals are not compelled to undergo a needless repetition of births and rebirths during this waiting period, but, instead, they spend the period on some exalted plane on which they come in contact with advanced souls and higher beings who act as their teachers. In some cases these advanced individuals consent to return to earth-life as great teachers, in order to aid in the general progress of the sub-race. The teaching is that among us today many of such advanced and self-sacrificing souls are dwelling, aiding in the general uplift.

The Rosicrucian teachings concerning the value of experiences in each earth-life are well illustrated by the following quotation from a leading writer, who says: "Many object to the doctrine of Re-Birth on the ground that the experiences of each life, not being remembered, must be useless and without value. This is an erroneous view of the subject, for while such experiences may not be fully remembered, yet they are not lost to us at all, but really form a part of the material of which our minds are composed. They exist in essence in the form of feelings, characteristics, inclinations, likes and dislikes, affinities, attractions, repulsions, etc., and are in this form just as much in evidence in our lives as are the experiences of yesterday which are well remembered. Look back over the years of your present life, and try to recall the experiences of one year ago, five years ago, ten years, twenty years, thirty years, and as much further back as you care to go. You will find that you can remember but few of the events of your life. The experiences of most of the days in which you have lived have been almost completely forgotten. Though these experiences may have seemed very vivid and real to you when they occurred, still they have faded into nothingness now, and they are to all intents and purposes lost to you.

But they are not lost! Remember, you are what you are today by reason of these very experiences which you now fail to remember—they exist in your character and have helped to mould and shape it. The apparently forgotten pains, pleasures, sorrows, and happinesses are active factors in the formation and maintenance of your character of today. This trial strengthened you along certain lines; that one changed your point of view and made you see things with a broader vision. This grief caused you to feel the pain of others; that disappointment spurred you on to new endeavors. And each and every one of them left a permanent mark upon your personality—upon your character. All men and women are what they are by reason of what they have gone through—have lived out and outlived. And though these happenings, scenes, circumstances, occurrences, experiences, have faded from the memory, their effects are indelibly imprinted upon the fabric of the character, and the individual of today is different from what he would have been had the happenings or experience not entered into his life.

"And this same rule applies to the characteristics brought over from past incarnations. You have not the memory of the experiences, but you have the fruit in the shape of characteristics, tastes, inclinations, etc. You have a tendency toward certain things, and a distaste for others. Certain things attract you, while other things repel you. All of these things are the result of your experiences in former incarnations. Your very tastes and inclination toward the study of the occult which are now causing you to read these lines, they are your legacy from some former life in which some seed-thoughts of esoteric teaching were dropped into your thought by some teacher or friend, and then aroused your interest and attracted your attention. You learned some little about the subject then—perhaps much—and developed a desire for more knowledge along these lines, which, manifesting in your present life has again brought you in contact with similar teachings. The same inclination will lead to further advancement along these lines in this life, and still greater opportunities in future incarnations. Nearly everyone who reads these lines will feel that much of the occult teaching now being received is but a 're-learning' of something previously known, although many of the things now taught have never been heard before in this life. You pick up a book and read something, and know at once that it is so, because in some vague way you have the consciousness of having studied and worked out the problem in some past life. All this is in accordance with the Law of Attraction which has caused you to attract that toward you for which you have an affinity, and which also causes others to be attracted to you. In the same way, and from the same cause, are the many reunions in this life of persons who have been related to each other in previous lives. The old loves, the old hates, work out in the new lives. We are bound to those whom we have loved, and also to those whom we have injured. The story must be worked out to the last chapter, although an increasing knowledge of the 'why and wherefore' of such things may relieve one of many entangling attachments and relationships of this kind.''

The Life After Death

The body of the Rosicrucian teachings includes very close and detailed instruction concerning the life of the soul between incarnations, the phenomena of the Astral World, and similar subjects, which would require many large books to record. In the present chapter we shall attempt to present to the student a general idea of the teachings concerning such subjects, without going into details which cannot be presented at the present time in the space at our command.

The moment of "death" arriving for the person, the soul sloughs off the ordinary physical body, and clad in the garments of the Elemental Soul it leaves the scene of the physical body. At first, however, the separation is not complete, for the Elemental Soul is still attached to the physical body by a thin slender thread or cord, which finally breaks and allows the soul to proceed on its way. The garments of the Elemental Soul are of course, in a sense, "physical" just as truly as were the garments of the visible body which were just cast off by the soul. In these new garments, however, the person is invisible to the ordinary sight of men, and except in the case of clairvoyants its presence cannot be detected.

The disembodied soul passes then on to what occultists know as the Astral Plane, which however is not a place in any sense of the word, but is rather "a state or condition of being" having nothing to do with space limitations. The Astral Plane manifests its phenomena by means of a higher rate of vibrations than those concerned in the phenomena of the Earth Plane. Different planes of being may occupy the same space at the same time without interfering one with the other.

Reaching the vibrations of the Astral Plane, the newly disembodied soul falls into a deep sleep, or state of coma, resembling the condition of the unborn child for several months before its birth. This condition is necessary in order to prepare the soul for its life on the new plane. The soul which has left the earth scene with calmness and peaceful mental attitude soon drops into a dreamless slumber; but those whose minds have been filled with strong desires connected with earth life often experience what are called "astral dreams" in which they revisit the scenes of earth life, and if possible may indulge in more or less distorted and dreamy communications through "mediums" and others. The strong desires and grief on the part of those left behind on the earth scenes, also, sometimes act to set up a "rapport" condition, and thus disturb the sleeping soul and interfere with its needed preparatory rest. In this slumber state the disembodied soul is fully protected from the influence or presence of other beings, and is as secure as is the child in its mother's womb.

Some souls require a long period of soul sleep on the Astral Plane before awakening into new activities, while others require only a comparatively short time. The general rule is that the higher the spiritual development of the soul, the longer is its period of soul sleep. The period of soul-sleep bears a close relation to the period of the sojourn of the soul on the Astral Plane—the less developed souls rushing speedily to rebirth while the more developed ones spend a much longer time on the Astral Plane between births.

In the soul sleep a strange process occurs, namely, the preparation for the sloughing off of the lower sheaths of the soul, leaving it free to enter the life on the Astral Plane clad only in the garments of its highest stage of spiritual attainment reached by it. Each soul awakens on the Astral Plane prepared to dwell on the plane of its highest and best, leaving the rest behind it. It awakens on the plane in which the highest and best in itself is given a chance to develop and expand, and to make progress, for the soul may, and does, make great progress in these between-births sojourns on the Astral Plane.

On the Astral Plane there are countless sub-planes, and divisions thereof, all of which are more or less independent of each other. The distinctions between the planes are altogether the result of differences on the rate of vibrations, and do not represent distances in space. Each sub-plane or division thereof is inhabited by souls exactly fitted to dwell upon it, by reason of their respective degree of spiritual unfoldment. The great law of attraction operates in producing this result, and each soul "feels perfectly at home" on the plane in which it finds itself. The law works with unerring accuracy, and makes no mistakes.

By certain fixed natural laws each soul is restricted to the realms of its own sub-plane or division of the Astral Plane, except that it may, if it desires, visit the planes beneath its own—but it cannot visit those higher than its own. The law of vibrations acts as the astral policemen in these matters. Disembodied souls may thus communicate with and have converse and association with each other, but only by the higher soul visiting the lower, and never the reverse.

The "scenery" and environment of the various sub-planes of the Astral Plane correspond with the ideas and beliefs of the souls occupying them. The Indian may find his "happy hunting ground" much more truly than some people would have us think. The thoughts and ideals of the soul is reflected upon the receptive substance of the Astral Plane, and each soul, in a certain sense, is the creator of its own environment and world—by its thought forms it builds itself a congenial world.

The soul makes progress during its sojourn on the Astral Plane, and prepares itself for a better and happier environment upon rebirth. During that sojourn it assimilates and digests the experiences of its last earth life, and learns the true lessons of such experiences, and these are reflected in the new character which it is forming. Past mistakes are seen, and the true meaning of many puzzling experiences are perceived. The soul thus "takes stock" of itself and is better prepared to meet the conditions of its next earth life.

On the Astral Plane the soul also receives the aid and assistance of some of the great spiritual teachers of the race, whose chosen occupation is to administer to the wants of the pained and suffering souls who are striving to find the way out of their troubles and mistakes. Not only do these teachers administer to the strictly spiritual wants of the souls seeking their help, but in many cases the soul is given the advantage of great assistance in chosen occupations, such as art, science, music, invention, etc., from advanced congenial souls ready and willing to help strugglers on the path. Many an artist, musician, writer, or inventory has come into rebirth greatly benefited and improved by reason of contact with such helpers of the Astral Plane.

Finally, after the longer or short period of sojourn of the soul upon the Astral Plane—the duration of which depends upon the degree of spiritual development of the soul—there comes to it the first dawn of a new state or condition, known to occultists as "the second soul-sleep," or slumber, in which the soul is prepared for its new birth on earth which is coming to it. A writer has well described this state as follows: "The second soul-sleep is preceded by a transition state of gradually declining activity and consciousness, and a corresponding desire for rest on the part of the soul. The natural processes of the Astral Plane nearing their close, the soul begins to experience a feeling of lassitude and weariness, and instinctively longs for rest and repose. It finds that it has lived out the greater part of its desires, ambitions, and ideals, and in many cases has also outlived them. There comes to it a wistful feeling of having fulfilled the purpose of its destiny, and a premonition of the coming of some newer phase of existence. The soul does not feel pain at the approach of the second soul-sleep, but, on the contrary, experiences satisfaction and happiness at the coming of something which promises rest and recuperation. Like the weary traveller who has climbed the mountain paths, and has delighted in the experiences of the journey, the soul feels that it has well earned a restful repose, and, like that traveller, it looks forward to the same with longing and desire."

The same writer says: "The soul may have passed by a few years, or perhaps a hundred or a thousand years, of earth-time, on the Astral Plane, according to its degree of development and unfoldment. But, be its stay short or long, the feeling of weariness reaches it at last, and, like many aged persons in earth-life, it feels that 'my work is over—let me pass on.' So sooner or later the soul feels a desire to gain new experience, and to manifest in a new life some of the advancement which has come to it by reason of its unfoldment on the Astral Plane. And, from these reasons, and also from the attraction of the desires which have been smouldering there, not lived out or cast off; or, possibly influenced by the fact that some loved soul, on a lower plane, is ready to reincarnate, and wishing to be with that soul (which is also a form of desire) the soul falls into a current sweeping toward rebirth and the selection of proper parents and advantageous environment. In consequence whereof it again falls into a state of soul-slumber, gradually, and so when its time comes it 'dies' on the Astral Plane, as it did before on the material plane, and passes forward toward rebirth on earth.''

There is another fact concerned with the awakening of the soul at rebirth, however, which is seldom mentioned by writers upon the subject, and which is consequently not known to many persons familiar with the other facts concerning rebirth. This fact is as follows: Strictly speaking, the soul continues in a condition of partial slumber even after it has been re-born in earth life. It does not fully awaken at once in the body of the new-born child in which it has been reincarnated, but on the contrary it awakens only gradually during the early childhood and youth of the child.

A writer, speaking of the above important fact concerning rebirth, says: "A soul does not fully awaken from its second soul-slumber immediately upon rebirth, but exists in a dream-like state during the days of infancy, its gradual awakening being evidenced by the growing intelligence of the babe, the brain of the child keeping pace with the demands made upon it. In some cases, however, the awakening is premature, and we see cases of prodigies, child-geniuses, etc., but such cases are more or less abnormal and unhealthy. Occasionally, the dreaming soul in the child half awakes, and startles its elders by some profound observation or mature remark or conduct. The rare instances of precocious children and infant genius are illustrations of cases in which the awakening has been more than ordinarily rapid. On the other hand, cases are known where the soul does not awaken as rapidly as the average, and the result is that the person does not show signs of full intellectual activity until nearly middle-aged. Cases are known where men seem to 'wake up' when they are forty years of age, or even older, and then take on freshened activity and energy, surprising those who had known them before.''

Here we ask the student to carefully consider another point concerning the need of and consequences of the second soul-slumber. Just as in the first soul-slumber the soul underwent a period of spiritual digestion and assimilation of the experiences of its earth-life, so in the second soul-slumber it undergoes a period of digestion and assimilation of its experiences on the Astral Plane. In both of these periods of spiritual digestion and assimilation the soul converts the substance of the experience into the solid flesh, bone, and blood of its ''character.'' It has outlived many things during its sojourn on the Astral Plane, and has left many undesirable qualities behind it.

In moving on toward rebirth during the second soul-slumber each soul goes to where it belongs, by reason of what it is. There is no favoritism shown, nor any injustice done it. The soul is not forced to reincarnate against its desires—in fact, it reincarnates because of its unsatisfied desires. It is carried into the current of rebirth because its tastes and desires have created bonds of attractions between it and the things of earth. These desires and tastes can be satisfied only through another experience of earth-life, amidst environment and conditions best suited to allow it to manifest those desires and tastes. It hungers to satisfy its desires and longings, and it moves in the direction in which such satisfaction is possible. Desire is always the great motive power of the soul in determining the conditions of rebirth, and the very fact of rebirth itself.

A writer on the subject has well said: ''The soul, preserving its desire for material things—the things of flesh and material life—and not being able to divorce itself from these things, will naturally fall into the current of rebirth which will lead it toward conditions in which these desires will flourish and become manifest. It is only when the soul, by means of many earth-lives, begins to see the worthlessness and illusory nature of earthly desires, and it begins to become attracted by the things of the life of its higher nature, and, escaping the flowing currents of earthly rebirth, it rises above them and is carried to' higher spheres. The average person, after years of earthly experience, is apt to say that he or she has no more desire for earth life, and that his or her only desire is to leave the same behind forever. These persons are perfectly sincere in their statements and beliefs, but a glance into their inmost souls would reveal an entirely different state of affairs. They are not, as a rule, really tired of earth life, but are merely tired of **the particular kind** of earth life which they have experienced during that incarnation. They have discovered the illusory nature of a certain set of earthly experiences, and feel disgusted at the same. But they are still full of another set of experiences on earth. They have failed to find happiness or satisfaction in their own experience, but they will admit, if they are honest with themselves, that if they could have had things 'just so and so,' instead of 'thus and so,' they would have found happiness and satisfaction. The 'if' may have been satisfied love, wealth, fame, gratified ambition, success of various kinds, etc.,—but be it what it may, the **'if'** is nearly always there. And that IF is really the seed of their remaining desires. And the longing for that IF is really the motive for rebirth. Very few persons would care to live over their earth life in the same way. But, like old Omar, they would be perfectly willing to remake the world according to their heart's desire, and then live the earth life. It is really not the earth life at all which is distasteful to them, but merely the particular experiences of earth life which are disdained. Give to the average man and woman youth, health, wealth, talent and love, and they will be very willing to begin the round of earth life afresh. It is only the absence of, or failure in, these or similar things, which causes them to feel that life is a failure, and a thing to be joyfully left behind. The soul, in its sojourn upon the Astral Plane, is rested, refreshed and reinvigorated. It has forgotten the weariness of life which it had experienced during the previous incarnation. It is again young, hopeful, vigorous, and ambitious. It feels within itself the call to action—the urge of unfulfilled desires, aspirations, and ambitions—and it readily falls into the currents which lead it to the scene of action in which these desires, are manifested.''

The same writer also says: ''Another point which should be cleared up is that regarding the character of the desires which serve as the motive power for rebirth. It is not meant that these desires are necessarily low or unworthy desires or longings. On the contrary, they may be of the highest character, and might be more properly styled aspirations, ambitions, or high aims, but the principle of desire is in them all. Desires, high and low, are the seeds of action. And the impulse toward action is always the distinguishing feature of desire. Desire always wants to **have** things, or to **do** things, or to **be** things. Love, even of the most unselfish kind, is a form of desire; so is aspiration of the noblest kind. A desire to benefit others is as much a desire as its opposite. In fact, many unselfish souls are drawn back into rebirth simply by the insistent aspiration to accomplish some great work for the race, or to serve others, or to fulfill some duty inspired by love. But, high or low, if these desires are connected in any way with the things of earth, they are rebirth motives and rudders. But in conclusion, let us say that no soul which does not in its inmost soul desire to be reborn on earth will ever be so reborn. Such a soul is attracted toward other spheres, where the attractions of earth exist not. In that case, the law of attraction carries the soul away from earth, not toward it. There are many souls which are now on the Astral Plane, undergoing the final stages of the casting off of the earthly bonds. And there are many souls now in earth life which will never again return to earth, but which after their next sojourn on the Astral Plane will rise to the higher planes of existence, leaving the earth and all earthly things behind forever. At the present time we are nearing the end of a cycle in which a very great number of souls are preparing for their upward flight, and many who read these lines may be well advanced in that cyclic movement.''

PART XI

THE SOUL'S PROGRESS

A very important point in the Rosicrucian teaching is that in which we are informed that the evolution of man is not confined to this planet, the earth, but rather is extended to a chain of seven planets. The Rosicrucians teach that the evolutionary processes of this planet are linked with and blended into the evolutionary processes of six other planets; and that life on this planet is likewise linked with and blended into the life on the six other planets of our planetary chain.

The Rosicrucians teach that these seven planets of our planetary chain are closely linked and connected by subtle etheric forces, and that there is a constant etheric current passing from one to the others and flowing ever through the entire circuit. These connected planets constitute the chain of worlds which is the series of homes of the individual soul, and the circuit of which is travelled by all individual souls. Not only does each individual soul now on earth reincarnate a number of times on this planet, but in the course of the ages it progresses to the next highest planet, just as in ages past it has progressed from the next lowest one. And this round of the chain of planets has been made several times by the human race in some form of existence, and will be made again several times.

The planets of this chain of worlds are not identical in composition and nature with the earth; on the contrary there is a wide difference between the several planets in this respect. The earth is not the highest in development in this chain, but on the contrary is far down on the scale, although there are others still lower. The progress of the souls around this chain of worlds, however, is not merely like a circle in which the soul travels from the lowest to the highest, but is rather according to the plan of the spiral, in which the journey always returns to the starting point, but on a higher plane of activity.

This journey of the life forms from world to world has been in progress since the beginning of the present world period, and was made by the lower forms of life as they climed the spiral stairway of evolution. A writer on the subject has said of this point: "It is the spiral character of the progress accomplished by the life impulses that develop the various kingdoms of Nature which accounts for the gaps now observed in the animated forms which people the earth. The thread of a screw, which is a uniform inclined plane in reality, looks like a succession of steps when examined only along one line parallel to its axis. The spiritual monads, which are coming round the system on the animal level, pass on to other worlds when they have performed their turn of animal incarnation here. By the time they come again, they are ready for human incarnation, and there is no necessity now for the upward development of animal forms into human forms—these are already waiting for their spiritual tenants. But if we go back far enough, we come to a period at which there were no human forms ready developed on the earth. When spiritual monads, travelling on the earliest or lowest human level, were thus beginning to come round, their onward pressure in a world at that time containing none but animal forms provoked the improvement of the highest of these into the required form—the much talked of missing link. * * * The impulse to the new evolution of higher forms is really given by rushes of spiritual monads coming round the cycle in a state fit for the inhabitation of new forms. These superior life impulses burst the chrysallis of the older form on the planet they invade, and throw off an efflorescence of something higher. The forms which have gone on merely repeating themselves for millenniums start afresh into growth; with relative rapidity they rise through the intermediate into the higher forms, and then, as these in turn are multiplied with the vigor and rapidity of all new growths, they supply tenements of flesh for the spiritual entities coming round on that stage or plane of existence, and for the intermediate forms there are no longer any tenants offering. Inevitably they become extinct.''

The writer above quoted from also points out a very important point in the progress of the life forms from world to world, as follows: ''The tide of life—the wave of existence, the spiritual impulse, call it by what name we please—passes on from planet to planet by rushes, or gushes, not by an even continuous flow. For the momentary purpose of illustrating the idea in hand, the process may be compared to the filling of a series of holes or tubs sunk in the ground, such as may sometimes be seen at the mouths of feeble springs, and connected with each other by little surface channels. The stream from the spring, as it flows, is gathered up entirely in the beginning by the first hole, or tub A, and it is only when this is quite full that the continued inpouring of water from the spring causes that which it already contains to overflow into tub B. This in turn fills and overflows along the channel which leads to tub C, and so on. * * * It is manifest from what we have already said, and in order that the progress of organisms on globe A shall be accounted for, that the mineral kingdom will no more develop the vegetable kingdom on globe A until it receives an impulse from without, than the earth was able to develop man from the ape till it received an impulse from without. * * * The full development of the mineral epoch on globe A prepares the way for the vegetable development, and as soon as this begins the mineral life impulse overflows into globe B. Then when the vegetable development on globe A is complete, and the animal development begins, the vegetable life impulse overflows to globe B, and the mineral impulse passes on to globe C. Then finally, comes the human impulse on globe A. It is necessary at this point to guard against one misconception that might arise. There is a fact to be stated which has such an influence on the course of events, that, when it is realized, it will be seen that the life impulse has passed several times around the whole chain of worlds before the commencement of the human impulse on globe A. This fact is as follows: Each kingdom of evolution, vegetable, animal, and so on, is divided into several spiral layers. The spiritual monads— the individual atoms of that immense life impulse of which so much has been said—do not fully complete their mineral existence on globe A, then complete it on globe B, and so on. They pass several times round the whole circle as minerals, and then again several times round as vegetables, and several times as animals.''

Now, leaving behind us the consideration of the details of the progress of the lower live forms, let us consider the details of the progress of the human race. It has been seen that the great wave of human life forms flows around the planetary chain in great waves—in successive waves of progress. The successive waves are known by occultists under the name of "rounds." But, according to the rule "As in the great so in the small," we find a corresponding series of spirals in the progress of the human race during each of its several sojourns on the earth. That is to say, an individual soul arriving on earth in one of the rounds does not merely live out its life here, and then pass on to the next planet. On the contrary, it lives a number of lives on this planet, and among several races. There exists a spiral of races in earth life, through which the individual soul must live and work its way. The number of these races is of course seven, for seven is the number manifested in all of the great occult processes of the Cosmos. There are seven great rounds of human progress around the chain of worlds, and in each round there are seven races in which the individual soul must manifest. The present round of the human race is the fourth.

Each of the seven races of the present (fourth) round of the race occupies the earth for a great period of time. The majority of the human race now on earth belong to the fifth race, though there are some stragglers from the fourth race still dwelling on earth. Each of these seven great races of humanity are sub-divided into seven sub-races and each sub-race is divided into seven branches.

The period during which each great root race of the human race flourishes on earth is sharply marked off from that of the one succeeding it by great convulsions of Nature which destroy practically all traces of the preceding civilization, and which leave but few survivors thereof. A writer has said of this point of the occult teaching: "The periods of the great root races are divided from each other by great convulsions of Nature and by great geological changes. Europe was not in existence as a continent at the time the fourth race flourished. The continent on which the fourth race lived was not in existence at the time the third race flourished, and neither of the continents which were the great vortices of the civilizations of those two races are in existence now. Seven great continental cataclysms occur during the occupation of the earth by the human life-wave for one round period. Each race is cut off in this way at its appointed time, some survivors remaining in parts of the world, not the proper home of their race; but these, invariably in such cases, exhibiting a tendency to decay, and relapsing into barbarism with more or less rapidity."

The individuals of the First Race of the present (fourth) round of the human race on earth ranged from a gross type scarcely above the brutes up to a very barbarous type. These higher types reincarnated later as the higher individuals of the Second Race, the lower types of the First Race constituting the lower subdivisions of the Second Race; the rule being that the less advanced souls of any race incarnate as the lowest types of the next and higher race.

The Rosicrucian teachings have but comparatively little to say concerning the history of the peoples of the First Race and the Second Race, but from what is taught it may be gathered that these peoples were of a very low order of humanity—the types which we know as the Cave Dwellers, the Stone-age people, and the Fire-people, give us the nearest possible idea of what these First Race and Second Race people must have been like. There was apparently little or nothing of what we call "civilization" among these people, and they were apparently about on a level with the very lowest types known among mankind on earth today. The teachings, however, state that there were a few comparatively highly advanced souls in the latter days of the Second Race, who acted as the leaven for the great improvement which came with the Third Race.

The era of the Second Race terminated, as usual, with a cataclysm which destroyed the majority of the race, and which scattered its survivors among far distant lands. Then dawned the period of the Third Race, the seat of its greatest activity being laid in the continent of Lemuria, which was situated on that portion of the globe which now lies at the bottom of the Pacific Ocean, and parts of the Indian Ocean. The continent of Lemuria also included Australia, Australasia, and other Pacific Islands—these surviving portions being really the highest points of the continent of Lemuria, the lower portions of which were sunk beneath the waves ages ago.

A writer says of the character of the civilization of Lemuria: "Life in Lemuria is described as being principally concerned with the physical senses and sensual enjoyment, only a few developed souls having broken through the fetters of materiality and reached the beginnings of the mental and spiritual planes of life. Some few indeed made great progress and were saved from the general wreck in order to become the leaven which would lighten the mass of mankind during the next great cycle. These developed souls were the teachers of the new races, and were looked upon by the latter as gods and supernatural beings, and legends and traditions concerning them are still existent among the ancient peoples of our present day. Many of the myths of the ancient peoples arose in this way. The traditions are that just prior to the great cataclysm which destroyed the people of the Third Race, there was a body of the Chosen Ones which migrated from Lemuria to certain islands of the sea which are now part of the main land of India. These people formed the nucleus of the Occult Teachers of Lemuria, and they kept alight the Flame of Truth with which was lighted the torches of the Fourth Race—the Race of the Atlanteans.''

With the passing away of Lemuria—the home of the Third Race—there arose from the depths of the Atlantic Ocean the future home of the people of the Fourth Race—the continent of Atlantis. Atlantis was situated in the space now occupied by a portion of the Atlantic Ocean, beginning at what is now known as the Carribbean Sea, and extending over to the region now known as Africa. What we now know as Cuba and the West Indies were the highest points of the continent of Atlantis, the lower portions being now buried beneath the waves of the Atlantic Ocean.

The writer above quoted from, says of the civilization of Atlantis: ''The civilization of Atlantis was remarkable, and its people attained heights which seem almost incredible to even those familiar with the highest achievements of man of our own times. The Chosen Ones preserved from the cataclysm which destroyed Lemuria, and who lived to a remarkably old age, had stored up within their minds the wisdom and learning of the civilization which had been destroyed, and they thus gave the Atlanteans an enormous advantage at the start. They soon attained great advancement along all the lines of human endeavor. They perfected mechanical inventions and appliances, reaching far ahead of even our present attainments. In the field of electricity especially they reached the stages that our present race will reach not sooner than two or three hundred years from now. Along the line of occult attainment their progress was far beyond the dreams of the average man of our own race, and in fact from this arose one of the causes of their downfall, for they prostituted the power to base and selfish uses, and practiced black magic. And so the decline of Atlantis began. But the end did not come at once, or suddenly —it was gradual. The continent, and the surrounding islands gradually sunk beneath the waves of the Atlantic Ocean, the process occupying 10,000 years. The Greeks and the Romans of our own cycle had traditions regarding the sinking of the continent, but their knowledge referred only to the disappearance of the small remainder—certain islands—the continent itself having disappeared thousands of years before their time. It is recorded that the Egyptian priests had traditions that the continent itself had disappeared nine thousand years before their time.''

As in the case of the Chosen Ones of Lemuria, so was it with the Elect Ones of Atlantis who were taken away from the doomed land some time prior to its destruction. These advanced individuals of the race left their Atlantean homes and ''led by the spirit'' migrated to portions of what are now known as South America and Central America, then but islands of the sea. These people left the traces of their civilization in these lands, and our scientists discovering these wonders greatly at the evidences of the high culture shown in them. When the Fifth Race appeared, these brave and advanced souls became the teachers of the new race, and were afterwards remembered as "gods," and the heroes of mythology. The Fifth Race evolved rapidly, owing to the urge of the souls of the Atlanteans pressing forward for reembodiment, and human forms were born to supply the demand, the fertility of the new race being marked.

The writer previously referred to says of the survival of members of a disappearing race, and their influence on the life of the new race: "By means of the cataclysms the races of each cycle were wiped out when their time came, but the few elect or chosen ones, that is those who had manifested the right to become torch-bearers, were carried away to some favorable environment, where they became as leaven to the mass—as 'gods' to the new races that quickly appeared. It must be noted, however, that the chosen or elect ones were not the only ones saved from the destruction that overtook the majority of the race in these cataclysms. On the contrary, a few survivors were preserved, although driven away from their former homes, and reduced to 'first principles of living' in order to become the parents of the new race. The new races springing from the fittest of the survivors quickly formed sub-races, being composed of the better adapted souls seeking reincarnation, while the less fit sank into barbarism and showed evidences of decay. A remnant of these degraded human creatures, however, persist in incarnation for thousands of years, being composed of those souls not sufficiently advanced to take part in the life of the new races. These 'left overs' are in evidence in our own times in the cases of the Australian savages, the African Bushmen, and the Digger Indians, and others of a similar low order of development. In order to understand the advance of each race it must be remembered that the more advanced souls, after passing out of the body, have a much longer period of rest in the higher planes, and consequently do not present themselves for reincarnation until a period quite late as compared with the hasty reincarnation of the less advanced souls who are hurried back to rebirth by reason of the strong earthly attachment and desires. In this way it happens that the earlier races of each cycle are more primitive folk than those who follow them as the years roll by. The soul of an earth-bound person reincarnates in a few years, and sometimes in a few days, while the soul of an advanced man may repose and rest on the higher planes for centuries—nay, even for thousands of years, until the earth has reached a stage in which the appropriate environment may be afforded it.''

At the beginning of the period of the Fifth Race (the present race of man) there were born not only the beginning of the new sub-races which always spring into existence at the beginning of a new cycle, but there were also born the descendants of the Elect, saved from the destruction of Atlantis by having been led away from the scene of danger. The new races were the descendants of the scattered survivors of the Atlantean peoples—that is, of the common run of those peoples. But the Elect few were superior individuals of their race, and imparted to their descendants their knowledge and wisdom. By an understanding of this distinction, we are able to comprehend the fact that at the same time there existed hordes of people of the new races—more or less primitive and ignorant—and at other places certain advanced peoples like the ancient Egyptians, Persians, Chaldeans, Hindus, etc. These advanced peoples represented the advanced souls—the old souls, of the advanced individuals of the Lemurian and Atlantean civilizations.

The descendants of some of the higher individuals were afterward known as the Assyrians and the Babylonians. In due time there appeared the beginnings of the great Roman, Grecian, and Carthaginian peoples. Then came the fall of the ancient peoples, and the rise of new subdivisions of the race. The history of the race shows the existence and manifestation of the law of the rise and fall of nations. Regarding this phenomenon, Dr. Draper, in his "History of the Intellectual Development of Europe" well says:

"We are, as we often say, the creatures of circumstances. In that expression there is a higher philosophy than might at first appear. From this more accurate point of view we should therefore consider the course of these events, recognizing the principle that the affairs of men pass forward in a determinate way, expanding and unfolding themselves. And hence we see that the things of which we have spoken as if they were matters of choice, were in reality forced upon their apparent authors by the necessity of the times. But in truth they should be considered as the presentation of a certain phase of life which nations in their onward course sooner or later assume. To the individual, how well we know that a sober moderation of action, an appropriate gravity of demeanor, belonging to the mature period of life, change from the wanton willfulness of youth, which may be ushered in, or its beginnings marked by many accidental incidents; in one, perhaps, by domestic bereavements, in another by the loss of fortune, in a third by ill-health. We are correct enough in imputing to such trials the change of character; but we never deceive ourselves by supposing that it would have failed to take place had these incidents not occurred. There runs an irresistible destiny in the midst of these vicissitudes. There are analogies between the life of a nation, and that of an individual, who, though he may be in one respect the maker of his own fortunes, for happiness or for misery, for good or for evil, though he remains here or goes there as his inclinations prompt, though he does this or abstains from that as he chooses, is nevertheless held fast by an inexorable fate—a fate which brought him into the world involuntarily, so far as he was concerned, which presses him forward through a definite career, the stages of which are invariable,—infancy, childhood, youth, maturity, old age, with all their characteristic actions and passions,—and which removes him from the scene at the appointed time, in most cases against his will. So also is it with nations; the voluntary is only the outward semblance, covering but scarcely hiding the predetermined. Over the events of life we may have control, but none whatever over the law of progress. There is a geometry that applies to nations an equation of their curve of advance. That no mortal man can touch.''

Thus have risen and fallen the great nations of the past, and thus will rise and fall the great nations of the future—and the law holds equally true in the case of the great nations of the present. Even at the time of this writing great things are under way in the history of the nations of the present. Cosmic forces are at work under the thin disguise of the petty plans and ambitions of rulers and statesmen. Looking backward over any period of past history the careful historian is able to see clearly the rise and progress of mighty movements which swept along in their current the affairs of great nations; and the historians of the future will be able to discern precisely such great movements and forces when they look back to the history of today, our present time. And in each case it will become evident that the majority of the peoples involved in the struggles have had no clear perception of the great forces at work, or of the actual goal to which the great movements have tended.

Thus have risen and fallen the great empires of the past, the Egyptian, the Persian, the Chaldean, the Grecian, the Roman, and the rest, Caesar, Alexander, Charlemagne, Napoleon, and the rest have been but the puppets of Fate through and by means of which she has worked out the dictates of Destiny. Races and peoples now regarded as but little more than half-civilized will be the successors of the proud nations of today just as the half-civilized Gauls, Angles, and Germanics succeeded the proud civilizations of ancient Greece and Rome.

When a nation begins to decline it is because its more advanced souls have passed on, leaving only the less progressive souls behind to carry on the work of the sub-race. The advanced souls pass on to new scenes of activity, and even the backward ones are not permitted to lag very far behind for the continual change and the creation of new environments tend to reawaken sleeping energies and to stimulate the lagging ones to fresh endeavor and activity.

The following quotations from a celebrated occultist may prove of interest to the student in connection with the particular subjects considered in the present chapter:

"At the half-way point of the fourth round here the polar point of the whole seven-world period is ~~passed. From~~ this point outwards the spiritual ego ~~begins its real~~ struggle with body and mind to manifest its transcendental powers. In the fifth round ~~the struggle~~ continues, but the transcendental faculties are largely developed, though the struggle between these on the one hand with physical intellect and propensity is fiercer than ever, for the intellect of the fifth round as well as its spirituality is an advance on that of the fourth. In the sixth round humanity attains a degree of perfection both of body and soul, of intellect and spirituality, which ordinary mortals of the present epoch will not readily realize in their imaginations. The most supreme combinations of wisdom, goodness, and transcendental enlightenment which the world has ever seen or thought of will represent the ordinary type of manhood. Those faculties which now, in the rare efflorescence of a generation, enable some extraordinarily gifted persons to explore the mysteries of Nature and gather the knowledge of which some crumbs are now being offered to the ordinary world, will then be the common appanage of all. As to what the seventh round will be like, the most communicative occult teachers are solemnly silent. Mankind in the seventh round will be something altogether too Godlike for mankind in the fourth round to forecast its attributes."

"The earth, while at present inhabited by fourth-round humanity—by the wave of human life on its fourth journey round the circle of the worlds—nevertheless contains some few persons, few in relation to the total number, who properly speaking belong to the fifth round. Now, in the sense of the term at present employed, it must not be supposed that by any miraculous process any individual unit has actually travelled round the whole chain of worlds once more often than his compeers. Under the law by which the tide-wave of humanity progresses, it will be seen that this is impossible. Humanity has not yet paid its fifth visit even to the planet next in advance of our own. But individual monads may outstrip their companions as regards their individual development, and so become exactly as mankind generally will be when the fifth round has been fully evolved. A man born as an ordinary fourth round man may, by processes of occult training, convert himself into a man having all the attributes of a fifth-round man, and so become what we may call an artificial fifth rounder."

PART XII

THE AURA AND AURIC COLORS

One of the most interesting points of the Rosicrucian teachings to the average student is that which is concerned with the Aura, or Psychic Atmosphere of the Human Individual, and the Astral Colors which manifest in that Aura, and otherwise.

By "Aura" is meant "A subtle invisible emanation or exhalation creating an atmosphere around the person or thing emanating it"—at least this is the popular definition of the term. In occult writings and teachings, however, the term has a more special meaning, and is employed to indicate the "psychic atmosphere" surrounding each human individual, invisible to the ordinary sense of sight, but perceptible by clairvoyant vision.

The human aura is an emanation from the soul, or souls, or the person whom it surrounds. It is akin to the rays of the sun, or the fragrance of the flower. It is a form of energy rather than of matter, yet is possesses a certain substantiality which justifies some writers in treating it as being composed of a very subtle form of matter. The human aura is egg-shaped, and extends to an average distance of two or three feet from the body of the person emanating it.

The human aura is composed of numerous elements, some of a low and some of a high order, corresponding to the elements manifesting in the soul of the person. Just as the manifestations of the souls of different persons vary greatly one from the other, so do their auras vary in the same degree. An advanced occultist, with trained clairvoyant vision, is able to read the mental and emotional character of a person like an open book, by means of the appearance and coloring of his or her aura.

The lowest element in the human aura is that which occultists call the "physical emanation," which is almost colorless, and which is marked by minute and thin "streaks" or bristle-like marks standing out from the body like bristles on a brush. When the person is in good health these "bristles" stand out stiffly, while when the person is in poor health or is suffering from impaired vitality they droop like the soft hair on the coat of an animal. This element of the aura appears to detach minute particles of itself from the aura as the person moves about, and it is believed that it is by these particles that dogs and other animals are able to track persons—it is this which is the essence of the so-called "scent" followed by the animals mentioned.

Another low element in the human aura is that which may be called the auric element of "vital energy." This element is perceived by clairvoyants as having a very faint pinkish glow, sometimes filled with tiny sparks of vital magnetism if the person be very magnetic. It is occasionally visible to persons lacking clairvoyant vision, and appears to them in the form of vibrating air, similar to the heated air arising from a field on a very warm day, or from a heated stove.

Passing over several unimportant auric elements of a lower degree, the student is asked to consider the most interesting phenomena of the "auric colors" which represent the mental and emotional elements in the soul of the man or woman. These elements are the characteristic features of the aura when perceived by clairvoyant vision. The aura, seen in this way, presents the appearance of a luminous cloud composed of varied and shifting colors, extending in egg-shape to a distance of about two or three feet from the body, and gradually growing fainter toward its outward limits until it finally disappears.

Each one of the colors in the aura represents some particular thought, mental state, emotion of feeling in the soul of the person. It will be seen at once that there is an almost infinite variation and shading of these auric colors, owing to the complexity in the emotional states of the average person.

The following table of the Auric Colors will give you the key to the blending and shading in the luminous cloud composing the human aura.

Table of the Auric Colors

Black indicates hatred, malice, revenge, and similar low feelings.

Gray (bright shade) indicates selfishness; (ghastly shade) indicates fear and terror; (dark shade) indicates melancholy.

Green (bright live shade) indicates diplomacy, worldly wisdom, suavity, tact, politeness, and "polite deceit" in general; (dirty, muddy shade) indicates low deceit, low cunning falsehood, trickery of a low order; (dark, dull shade) indicates jealousy, envy, covetousness.

Red is the color of the passions in general, but there is a great variety in its manifestations, for instance: Red (dull and appearing as if mixed with smoke) indicates sensuality and the lower animal passions; Red (appearing as bright flashes, sometimes light lightning in form) indicates anger. In this case the red usually is shown on a black background when the anger arises from hatred or malice, and on a greenish background when the anger arises from jealousy, envy, etc., and without any background when the anger arises from "righteous indignation" and the defense of what is believed to be a righteous cause. Red (crimson shade) represents Love, and varies in shade according to the character of the passion named. For instance, a dull and heavy crimson shade indicates a gross, sensual love; while the brighter, clearer and more pleasing shades indicate love blended with higher feelings and accompanied by higher ideals; and the highest form of human love between the sexes manifests in a beautiful rose color.

Brown (reddish shade) indicates avarice and greed.

Orange (bright shade) represents pride and ambition.

Yellow, in its various shades, represents intellectual power in its various forms. A beautiful, clear, golden yellow indicates high intellectual attainment, logical reasoning, unprejudiced judgment and discrimination. A dark dull yellow shade indicates intellectual power contenting itself with thoughts and subjects of a low, selfish order. The shade between the two just indicated denote the presence of higher or lower thought, respectively, the dark representing the lower, and the light the higher.

Blue (dark shade) represents religious emotion, feeling, and tendencies in general. The dull shades, however, indicate religious emotion of a low order, while the clearer brighter shades indicate religious emotions of a high order. These shades vary and range from a dull indigo to a beautiful bright violet. **Light Blue** (of a peculiar hue and shade) indicates spirituality. This spiritual blue is of a peculiarly clear, transparent, and luminous appearance, which is difficult to describe in words. In the auras of some persons of a very high degree of spirituality there appear tiny luminous spark-like points, often twinkling and sparkling like the stars in the heavens on a clear night.

In addition to the ordinary colors named above, there are several shades which cannot be named, for they correspond to colors outside of the field of human vision, such as "infra red" and "ultra violet." Without going deeply into this phase of the subject, it may be said that the "ultra violet" auric colors denote high spiritual powers manifested in the direction of the highest and most worthy aims and ends; while the "infra red" auric colors denote psychic powers employed in unworthy ways and for base ends—as for instance, that which the occultists know as "black magic."

There are two other auric colors which are impossible to describe in words, for there are no terms adequate for such expression. These colors are as follows: (1) the true primary yellow, which indicates the highest spiritual illumination of the intellect; and (2) true pure white, or a peculiar brilliancy and transparency, which indicates the presence of the awakened spirit.

A writer on the subject has said of the manifestations of the auric colors: "Even when the mind is calm there hover in the aura the shades indicative of the predominant tendencies in the man, so that his stage of advancement and development, as well as his tastes and other features of his personality, may be readily discerned. When the mind is swept by a strong passion, feeling or emotion, the entire aura seems to be colored by the particular shade or shades representing it. For instance, a violent fit of anger causes the whole aura to show bright red flashes upon a black background, almost eclipsing the other colors. This state lasts for a longer or shorter time, according to the strength of the passion. If people could but have a glimpse of the human aura when so colored, they would become so horrified at the dreadful sight that they would never again permit themselves to fly into a rage—it resembles the flame and smoke of the 'pit' which is referred to in the orthodox churches, and, in fact, the human mind in such a condition becomes a veritable hell for the time being. A strong wave of love sweeping over the mind will cause the aura to show crimson, the shade depending upon the character of the passion. Likewise a burst of religious feeling will bestow upon the entire aura a blue tinge. In short, a strong emotion, feeling, or passion causes the entire aura to take on its color while the feeling lasts. You will see from what we have said that there are two aspects to the color feature of the aura, the first depending upon the predominant thoughts habitually manifesting in the mind of the person; the second depending upon the particular feeling, emotion or passion (if any) being manifested at that particular time. The passing color disappears when the feeling dies away, although a feeling, passion, or emotion repeatedly manifested shows itself in time upon the auric color. The habitual color shown in the aura, of course, changes gradually from time to time as the character of the person improves or changes.

The habitual colors shown indicate the 'general character' of the person; the passing colors show what feeling, emotion, or passion (if any) is dominating him at that particular time."

Another writer, describing the appearance of the aura of a person, has said: ''The shades and colors of the aura present an ever-changing kaleidoscopic spectacle. The trained occultist is able to read the character of any person, as well as the nature of his passing thoughts and feelings, by simply studying the shifting colors of his aura. To the developed occultist the mind and character becomes as an open book, to be studied carefully and intelligently. Even the student of occultism who has not been able to develop the clairvoyant vision to such a high degree, is soon able to develop the sense of psychic perception whereby he is able to at least 'feel' the vibrations of the aura, though he may not see the colors, and thus be able to interpret the mental states which have caused them. The principle of course is the same, as the colors are but the outward appearance of the vibrations themselves, just as the ordinary colors on the physical plane are merely the outward manifestations of vibrations of matter. But it must not be supposed that the human aura is always perceived in the appearance of a luminous cloud of ever-changing color. When we say that such is its characteristic appearance, we mean it in the same sense that we describe the ocean as a calm, deep body of greenish waters. We know, however, that at times the ocean presents no such appearance, but, instead, is seen as rising in great mountainous waves, white-capped, and threatening the tiny vessels of men with its power. Or again, we may define the word 'flame' in the sense of a steady, bright stream of burning gas, whereas, we know only too well that the word also indicates the great hot tongues of fiery force that stream out from the windows of a burning building and lick to destruction all with which it comes in contact. So it is with the human aura. At times it may be seen as a beautiful, calm, luminous atmosphere, presenting the appearance of a great opal under the rays of the sun. Again, it blazes like the flames of a great furnace, shooting forth great tongues of fire in this direction and that, rising and falling in great waves of emotional excitement, or passion, or perhaps whirling like a great fiery maelstrom toward its centre, or swirling in an outward movement away from its centre. Again, it may be seen as projecting from its depths smaller bodies or centres of mental vibration, which like sparks from a furnace detach themselves from the parent flame and travel far away in other directions—these are the projected thought forms of which all occultists are fond of speaking and which make plain many strange psychic occurrences.''

The Three Primary Auric Colors

Like their physical counterparts, the Auric Colors are derived from three Primary Colors, from which all the various combinations and colors are formed. These three primary colors, together with White and Black, give us the key to the entire auric spectrum.

The **Three Primary Colors** are as follows: (1) Red; (2) Blue; and (3) Yellow. From these three primary colors all others are formed by combinations and blendings, or by the addition of Black or White. Thus, the Secondary Colors are formed as follows: (1) Green, derived from a combination of Yellow and Blue; (2) Orange, derived from a combination of

Yellow and Red; (3) Purple, derived from a combination of Red and Blue. Further combinations produce other colors, for instance: Green and Purple form Olive; Orange and Purple form Russet; Green and Orange form Citrine.

Black is really an absence of color, while **White** is really a harmonious blending of all colors. The blending of the Primary Colors in varied proportions produce what are known as the "hues" of color; and adding White we obtain "tints," while mixing Black produces "shades."

Key to the Auric Colors

An understanding of the basic character of the Three Primary Auric Colors, and of Auric Black and Auric White, gives the student the key to the whole range of auric coloring. For this purpose the following table is presented:

The Red Group. Red represents the physical nature, and its presence always indicates the existence and activity of that part of the nature of man.

The Blue Group. Blue represents the religious, or spiritual nature, and its presence always indicates the existence and activity of that part of the nature of man.

The Yellow Group. Yellow represents the intellectual nature, and its presence always indicates the existence and activity of that part of the nature of man.

White. White represents Pure Spirit, and its presence always indicates the presence and activity of that Reality in the nature of man.

Black. Black represents the negation of Pure Spirit, and opposes it in every way, and its presence always indicates the existence and activity of this negative principle in the nature of man.

The various combinations of the three Primary Auric Colors are formed in connection with White and Black, as well as by the blending of the three themselves. These combinations of course result from the shades of mental and emotional activity manifested by the individual. But not only is the blending caused by the mixing of the colors themselves, in connection with Black and White, but in certain cases the body of one color is found to be streaked, striped, dotted, or clouded by other colors. At times there is perceived the mixture of two antagonistic color streams fighting against each other before blending. Again we see the effect of one color neutralizing another. In some cases great black clouds obscure the bright colors beneath, and then darken the fierce glow of color, just as is often witnessed in the case of a physical conflagration. Again, we find great flashes of bright yellow, or red, flaring across the field of the aura, showing agitation or the conflict of intellect and passion.

It should be noted by the student, in passing, that the Green group of auric colors seems, at first glance, to be an exception to the general rule regarding the blending of the primary auric colors; and to manifest contradictions in character. For instance, it is difficult for the average student to comprehend why a blending of the spiritual blue and the intellectual yellow should yield a green indicating deceit, etc. A subtle analysis of deceit, however, gives the secret of this combination, particularly when it is noted that in certain of the less desirable of the green combinations there is combined a slight mixture of black and of red. It is not necessary to go into details concerning this particular point—it is enough to indicate the nature of the solution of the mystery. Again, there is a certain shade of Green, that which manifests in the prevailing colors of trees, plants, etc., which when shown in the auric coloring indicates a love of nature, etc. The following words from a celebrated occultist gives a valuable hint to those whose minds tend to keen analysis concerning these matters; this occultist says: "To those who are fond of analysis of this kind, I will drop the following hint, which may help them in the matter, viz.: The key is found in the fact that Green lies in the centre of the spectrum, and is a balance between the two extremes, and is also influenced by these two extremes in a startling manner."

Important Suggestions

The Rosicrucian teachers do not content themselves with instructing their students concerning the particular colors which, when seen in the aura, indicate the presence and activity of certain mental or emotional states in the person. They also instruct the student according to the celebrated principle of Action and Reaction, which forms an important feature of certain branches of the Rosicrucian teachings. That is to say they instruct the student that if he will hold in his mind the mental image of a certain color, there will result a reaction in the direction of the production in the student's mind or emotional nature of the feeling or emotion corresponding to that particular color. For instance, if the student will hold his thought and attention firmly concentrated on the Red group of colors, there will be awakened in him a strong passional emotion, and the manifestation of animal vitality and vigor, virility, courage, etc. Again, if he will hold in his mind in the same way the Blue group of colors, he will experience an uplift of spiritual or religious emotional feelings, and his nature will be quickened along those lines. Again, if he would stimulate his intellectual faculties, or reinvigorate a tired mind, he has but to concentrate on the Yellow group of colors to obtain the desired result. So, it is seen, not only do mental and emotional states manifest appropriate colors, but the colors themselves tend to produce their corresponding mental and emotional states. The action of Red upon the bull and other animals is explained in this way; also we have here a suggestion as to why a man "sees red" under moments of great excitement leading to physical action of punishment, etc.

It is also a part of the teachings that the Three Primary Colors have a decided therapeutic effect, and that one may apply the principle in healing work. The colors may be applied either by means of physical colors placed in the environment of the person, or else held in the mind of the mental healer giving the treatment. Here is the Therapeutic Scale of Colors:

Therapeutic Scale of Colors

Blues, Violet, Lavender, etc., have a cooling and soothing effect upon the nervous system, and upon the blood and bodily organs.

Grass Greens, have a resting and invigorating effect upon the same.

Yellows and Orange have an inspiring and illuminating effect upon the mental faculties.

Reds have an exciting and stimulating effect upon mind and body (this is particularly true of scarlets and other bright reds).

The Protective Aura

The Rosicrucian teachers also instruct their pupils in the matter of the creation and maintenance of The Protective Aura, which is a shelter of soul, mind, and body against evil influences directed against them consciously or unconsciously. This Protective Aura is an effective armor against all forms of psychic attack and invasion, no matter from whom they emanate. It affords a simple but very powerful and efficient means of protection against adverse psychic influences, "malicious mental magnetism," black magic, etc., and is also a protection against psychic vampirism or the draining of magnetic strength.

The method of forming the Protective Aura is very simple. It consists merely of the formation of a mental image (accompanied by a demand of the will) of yourself as being surrounded by an aura of Pure Clear White Light—the symbol and indication of Spirit. A little practice will enable you to actually feel the presence and power of this Protective Aura. The White Light is the radiation of Spirit, and Spirit is master of All Things. As a teacher has said: "The highest and deepest occult teaching is that the White Light must never be used for purpose of attack or personal gain, but that it may properly be employed by anyone, at any time, to protect himself or herself against adverse outside psychic influences no matter by whom exerted. It is the armor of the soul, and may well be employed in such way whenever or wherever the need arises."

In the explanation given here concerning the aura will be found a key to very interesting phenomena along the lines of Personal Magnetism, Magnetic Influence, Personal Atmosphere, etc.

PART XIII

THE SEVEN COSMIC PRINCIPLES

The Rosicrucians teach that there are Seven Cosmic Principles present and operating throughout the Cosmos, and extending even to its smallest activities. These Seven Cosmic Principles are as follows:

I. The Principle of Correspondence.
II. The Principle of Law and Order.
III. The Principle of Vibration.
IV. The Principle of Rhythm.
V. The Principle of Cycles.
VI. The Principle of Polarity.
VII. The Principle of Sex.

The student is now asked to consider each of the above stated Cosmic Principles in detail.

I. The Principle of Correspondence

The Principle of Correspondence manifests in a certain correspondence or analogy or agreement between manifestations of the various planes of activity in the Cosmos. It is indicated by the old Hermetic aphorism: "As above, so below; as below, so above," and by the Arcane axiom: "Ex Uno disce Omnes," or "From One know All." The Rosicrucians, and other ancient occultists, hold that the laws governing the nature and activity of the amoeba, likewise govern the nature and activity of man and beings higher than man. What is true of matter is true of energy and of mind. The occultists make a practical application of this universal principle, in the direction of studying the unknown by means of the known, with the knowledge that the same laws govern each. Thus, just as the solar system may be known by means of studying the atoms and molecules, so may the higher planes of being be studied by an examination of the lower planes in manifestation before us.

After discovering the operation of certain principles in one thing we may safely reason by analogy based upon the assumption that these principles exist in other things on a higher plane, and thus discover the nature of the unknown "x." Thus the occultist reasons that there is Law and Order manifest on every plane of being; that there is a Principle of Vibration manifest on every plane of being; that there is a Principle of Rhythm manifest on every plane of being; that there is a Principle of Cycles manifest on every plane of being; that there is a Principle of Polarity manifest on every plane of being; that there is a Principle of Sex manifest on every plane of being. And the further that human investigation is pushed into the Unknown, the greater is the proof of the existence of these Cosmic Principles reasoned out by the ancient occultists upon the fundamental basis of the Principle of Correspondence.

A writer has said of this Cosmic Principle: "There is always a correspondence between the laws and phenomena of the various planes of life and being. The grasping of this truth gives one the means of solving many a dark paradox, many a hidden secret of Nature. There are planes beyond our knowing, but when we apply the Principle of Correspondence to them we are able to understand much that otherwise would be unknowable to us. This principle is of universal application and manifestation, on the various planes of the material, mental and spiritual universe—it is an universal law. The ancient Hermetists considered this principle as one of the most important mental instruments by which man was able to pry aside the obstructions which hid from view the Unknown. Its use even tore aside the Veil of Isis to the extent that a glimpse of the face of the goddess might be caught. Just as a knowledge of the principles of Geometry enables a man to measure distant suns and their movements, while seated in an observatory, so a knowledge of the Principle of Correspondence enables man to reason intelligently from the Known to the Unknown. Studying the moneron, he understands the archangel.

Without going deeply into the matter of the application of this particular Cosmic Principle, we may say that one of the fundamental facts of being discovered by the ancient occultists by the application of the said principle is this: That in every thing there is to be found (1) Substance, or Body; (2) Motion or Active Energy; and (3) Consciousness or Awareness. Therefore, when dealing with planes of being of which, at the time, they had but little knowledge, the ancient occultists always assumed the existence in everything on the unknown plane of these three great forms of manifestation. And all future esoteric investigation and discovery tended to disclose facts corroborating and sustaining the original assumption derived by analogy, and the discoveries of modern science have invariably tended in the same direction. It may be interesting to take a hasty glance at the presence of these three forms of manifestation, as follows:

Substance. The ancient occult teaching that "Everything has body" seems to be fully corroborated by all subsequent investigation. But it must be noted that by "substance" or "body" is not necessarily meant what modern science calls "matter," for the latter is merely one form or phase of "substance" or "body." Matter, as we know it, has a great range of manifestation, within the limits of which are found the hardest granite or steel or diamond, as well as the finest and most subtle and tenuous gases. The discovery by science of what it calls "radiant matter" opens out a field to science previously tilled only by the occultists and metaphysicians. Such matter is really not "matter" at all, but "super-matter," and a higher form of "substance" or "body," But, known to the occultists, there are forms of "substance" or "body" as much finer and rarer than radiant matter as the latter is rarer and finer than the granite, steel, or diamond. Even the hypothetical Ether of science is gross by comparison with some of the forms and phases of "substance" or "body" known to the occultists and alchemists. As a writer has said: "The field of matter, as known to science, as compared with the real extent of the Principle of Substance, is as no more than a hair-line drawn across a yard-stick." The occult teachings inform us that there are living beings in existence on other planes whose bodies are composed of substance so fine and subtle that the term "ethereal" is the only one to be even fairly adequate to be employed in connection with them. Remember, the occult teaching is that "**Everything**

has substance or body." And "everything" includes All-that-is-Manifest.

Motion or Active Energy. The ancient occult teaching that "Everything moves" seems to be fully corroborated by all subsequent investigation. Motion, of course, results from the presence and power of Active Energy. And Active Energy is found everywhere present and in manifestation. Both the occult teaching and modern science teach that everything is undergoing constant change, and change is impossible without active energy and motion. Active Energy manifests through gravitation, cohesion, chemical affinity, electronic attraction, expansion, contraction, centrifugal and centripetal force, light, heat, magnetism, electricity, etc., etc. And there are much finer forces than these known to the occultists, though not as yet discovered by science. Wherever there is Substance there is Motion. Nothing is at absolute Rest. Everything Moves. From the tiniest electron or atom, up to the greatest sun, all is in constant motion. Remember, the occult teaching is that **"Everything moves."** And "everything" includes All-that-is-Manifest.

Consciousness. The ancient occult teaching that "Everything is aware" seems to be fully corroborated by all subsequent investigations. As we have seen in the study of the chapters concerning the Planes of Consciousness, there is manifested consciousness of some form, phase, or degree on all planes of life and being. Wherever there is Substance there is also Motion, and also Consciousness. Substance, Consciousness, and Motion are always found together—never apart or divorced one from another. There can be no Substance without Consciousness and Motion; no Motion without Substance and Consciousness; and no Consciousness without Substance and Motion.

In the above we have but one of the many applications of the Principle of Correspondence, which teaches that "As above, so below; as below, so above;" and that "From One know All."

II. The Principle of Law and Order

The Principle of Law and Order manifests in the presence and manifestation of a regular sequence, and orderly procession of phenomena in the universe of things. It is voiced by the celebrated axiom of a leading scientist that "The Universe is governed by laws." The spirit of this principle of truth is embodied in the very term "The Cosmos," which term is derived from the Greek term "Kosmos," meaning: "The world or universe considered in connection with perfect order and arrangement, as opposed to Chaos."

In the occult teachings of the Rosicrucians it is impressed upon the student that "there is no such thing as Chance," in so far as Chance is used in the sense of "uncaused happening." The student is taught that even in the instances in which Blind Chance seems to rule, there is still the manifestation of Law and Order and Causation, though the Causes may lie outside of human knowledge. The term "Chance" is now employed by careful thinkers only in the sense of "The unknown, or unforeseen cause or causes of an event."

In the Cosmos the same Causes, manifesting under the same circumstances always produce the same Effects. All of our science and thought is based upon this universal fact, and intelligent reasoning would be impossible without the tacit assumption of the truth of this principle. There is no room for Chance or haphazard, lawless happenings in the Cosmos. Everything, every happening, and every event, must have its "causes" and its "becauses." Everything happens "because" of so-and-so. Given certain causes, there must ensue certain results and effects. "Nothing ever happens" says the old proverb—and nothing ever does "happen" except for definite causes, and in pursuance with universal laws. As someone has said: "There is no room in the universe for anything outside of and independent of Law and Order. The existence of such an outside Something would render all Cosmic Law ineffective, and would plunge the universe into chaotic disorder and lawlessness."

A writer has said regarding this: "A careful examination will show that what we call 'Chance' is merely the idea of obscure causes, causes that we cannot understand. The word 'Chance' is derived from a word meaning "to fall" (as the falling of dice from the box onto the board), the essence of the idea being that the fall of the dice are merely 'happenings' unrelated to any cause. And this is the sense in which the term is generally employed. But when the matter is closely examined it is seen that there is no chance whatsoever about the fall of the dice. Each time a die falls, and displays a certain number, it obeys a law as infallible as that which governs the revolution of the planets around the sun, and the movement of the sun itself. Back of the fall of the die are causes, or chains of causes, running back further than the mind can follow. The position of the die in the box; the amount of muscular energy expended in the throw; the condition of the table; etc., etc., all are causes, the effect of the combination of which may be seen in the fall and position of rest of the die. But back of these perceived causes there are chains of unseen preceding causes, all of which have had a bearing upon the position of the die as it comes to rest on the table. If the die be cast a great number of times, it will be found that the numbers shown will be about equal, that is, there will be an equal number of one-spot, two-spots, etc., coming uppermost. Toss a penny in the air, and it may come down either 'heads' or 'tails.' But make a sufficient number of tosses, and the heads and tails will even up. This is the operation of the Law of Average. But both the average and the single toss come under the Law of Cause and Effect.''

The same writer says: ''There is no original happening; and every happening is merely a link in a great chain of happenings. There is a continuity between precedent happenings, the present happenings, and future happenings. There is always the relation between what has gone before, and what is happening now, and what will happen in the future. For instance: A stone is dislodged from the mountain-side and crashes through the roof of a cottage in the valley below. At first sight this seems to be a chance effect, but when we examine the matter we find a great chain of causes behind it. In the first place, there was the rain which softened the earth supporting the stone and which allowed or 'caused' it to fall. Then back of that there was the influence of the sun, other rains, etc., which gradually disintegrated the rock from a larger piece. Then there were the causes which led to the formation of the mountain, and its upheaval by convulsions of nature, and so on ad infinitum. We might follow up the causes behind the rain. Then we might consider the existence of the cottage just at that place at that particular moment. In short we would soon find ourselves involved in a mesh of cause and effect from which we would soon strive vainly to extricate ourselves.''

But the Rosicrucians do not believe in Fatalism in the ordinary sense of that term. Fatalism denies that preceding events have any causal relation to preceding events, and holds that the fated event would have happened in spite of any precedent event. Fatalism makes the fated event stand apart from the Law of Cause and Effect, and implies that the event arose from the operation of some arbitrary degree or will. The following quotation from an authoritative source will serve to point out the essential distinction between Fatalism and the Determination of Cosmic Law:

"Fatalism is the doctrine that the course of events is so determined that what an individual wills can have no effect on that course. Fatalism must be carefully distinguished from Determinism, as the confusion of these two conceptions has been responsible for much of the popular prejudice existing against Determinism. Fatalism, as has been said, denies that Will has efficacy in shaping events. Determinism maintains that this causally efficient Will is itself to be causally accounted for; this is entirely different for the fatalistic assertion that Will counts for nothing. In fact Determinism and Fatalism are fundamental antagonistic. Determinism asserts that events are determined by some of the events that immediately precede them; that if the latter were different the former would be different. Fatalism denies that immediately preceding events have anything to do with the origination of events immediately following: it asserts that the latter would occur even if the former were changed. To say that one's death is fixed by Fate is to deny that it takes place by natural law. Or, more accurately, it is to say that however much one varies the cause, one cannot vary the effect. The fatalist's position is that the **end** is predetermined, but not the **means**; the determinist's position is that the events now occurring lead by causality to other events, which are thus fixed because their causes are actually existent. Or, to put it still another way, for the fatalist what actually determines the event is not another event immediately preceding, but some mysterious decree issued by some mysterious agent ages before the event. This enables us to see that Fatalism gives no scope to the Will. But Determinism, which merely asserts that every event has its determining conditions in its immediate antecedents, includes among those antecedents the human Will. Thus Determinism is consistent with a belief in the efficacy of Will, and Fatalism is not.''

In the above we have illustrations of some of the many applications of the Principle of Law and Order, which teaches that ''Nothing happens by Chance, but everything happening is in accordance with Law,. Order, and Causation.''

III.   The Principle of Vibration

The Principle of Vibration manifests in the manifestation of a state of vibration in everything in the Manifested Cosmos. It is voiced by the old occult axiom: ''Everything vibrates.''

Modern science has advanced to the position of the ancient occultists who asserted that everything in the Cosmos was in a state or condition of continuous vibration. Science now tells us that not only is every particle of matter, or every mass of matter, in a state of continual vibration, but also that light, heat, magnetism, electricity and every other form of natural force results from a state of vibration.

The occultists go further than this, and assert that even on the mental and spiritual planes there is ever manifest a condition of vibration. In fact, the occultists teach that the distinction between the several planes of being is almost entirely due to the difference in the rate and character on the vibrations manifested. The difference between steel and gold, or diamond and clay is entirely a matter of difference in vibrations. All forms of energy are accompanied by distinctive degrees of vibrations. The conditions of material substances are created by the respective degree of vibrations manifested by each.

A writer has said: ''Science offers the illustration of a rapidly moving wheel, top, or cylinder, to show the effects of increasing rates of vibration. The illustration supposes a wheel, top, or revolving cylinder, running at a high rate of speed—we will call this revolving thing 'the object' in following out the illustration. Let us suppose the object to be moving slowly. It may be seen readily, but no sound of its movement reaches the ear. Then the speed is gradually increased. In a few moments the movement becomes so rapid that a deep growl or low note may be heard. Then as the rate of motion is increased the note rises higher in the musical scale. Then, the motion being still further increased, the next highest note is distinguished. Then, one after another, all the notes of the musical scale appear, rising higher and higher as the motion is increased.

Finally, when the motions have reached a certain rate, the final note perceptible to human ears is reached, and the shrill, piercing shriek dies away, and silence follows. No sound is then heard from the revolving object, for its rate of motion is so high that the human ear cannot register the vibrations. Then comes the perception of rising degrees of Heat. After quite a time in which degrees of heat are being manifested without any sign of distinguishable color (though certain colors are there, but imperceptible to human vision) there gradually is manifested a dull dark reddish color in the revolving object. As the rate of speed increases, the red becomes brighter. Then, as the speed is still further increased, the red changes into an orange color. Then follow, successively, the shades of green, blue, indigo, and finally violet, as the rate of vibrations increase. Then the violet fades away, and all color disappears, the human eye not being able to register them. But there are invisible rays emanating from the revolving object, the rays that are used in photographing, and other subtle rays of light. Then begin to be manifested the peculiar rays known as the 'X Rays,' etc., as the constitution of the object changes. Electricity and Magnetism are emitted when the appropriate rate of vibration is attained.

"When the revolving object reaches a certain degree or rate of vibration, its molecules disintegrate, and resolve themselves into the original elements or atoms. Then the atoms, in turn disintegrate, and are resolved into the countless corpuscles which constitute the atom. And finally even the corpuscles disintegrate, and a condition of ethereal substance is produced. Science does not dare to follow the illustration further, but the occultists teach that if the vibrations were continuously increased the revolving object would mount up the successive states of manifestation, and would display the various higher stages of consciousness.''

The occultists teach that each and every mental or emotional state has its own distinctive rate of vibration, and that the secret of ''emotional contagion'' is due to the fact that similar vibrations are set up in the emotional nature of persons subjected to the influence of strong emotion in another person. All manifestations of thought, emotion, will, desire, or feeling, or any other mental state, are accompanied and caused by vibrations of a certain high rate, and that these vibrations tend to influence others in their field of ''induction,'' and tend to set up in the others similar vibrations. In this fact lies the secret of Mental Influence, Personal Magnetism, etc. A knowledge and mastery of the science of mental vibrations enables the skilled Rosicrucian to change the rate of his mental vibrations at will, and to thus maintain a state of mental calm and power, unaffected by the thought vibrations of those around him.

So truly does advanced modern scientific thought recognize the nature of vibrations, that the axiom is announced that ''The difference in things consists entirely of difference in vibrations.'' This axiom is akin to the ancient occult aphorism that ''Things manifest differences according to their rate of vibrations.''

So, it is seen, all human investigation tends to prove the truth of the old occult axiom that ''Everything vibrates.''

IV. The Principle of Rhythm

The Principle of Rhythm manifests that universal regular swing or time-beat which is apparent in all the manifested world, from its highest to its lowest manifestation. The ancient occult axiom "Everything beats time" expresses this fundamental fact of the Cosmos.

Rhythm means: "Regularly recurring motion, change or impulse proceeding in time-measured, alternating sequence." The term "alternating" means "succeeding, acting or happening in turn." The term "recurring" means "returning repeatedly; occurring at stated intervals, or according to some regular rule."

Rhythm manifests in regular recurrence, succession in turn, repeated occurrence at stated intervals, etc. The simplest and most typical example or illustration of Rhythm is found in the swinging of the pendulum; the revolution of the earth on its axis, and around the sun, in regular measured time; the "beating time" of the metronome or the baton of the musical director; or the measured time in poetry or music. Rhythm means "beating time" in regular motion.

In all Rhythm there is recurring motion, change, and activity; action or motion in opposite directions; alternations between the opposite poles of action or motion; and a regular interval of time between the alternating actions or motions. In all phenomenal change or motion there is to be always found the existence of two opposite extremes between which the rhythmic change or motion is manifested. Rhythmic change and motion proceed by alternating swings between these two extremes, with a regular period of time elapsing between each beat, swing, or impulse in either direction. The period of "time" between the two alternating impulses constitutes the rhythmic rate, degree, or beat—its rhythmic measure of periodicity.

The term "periodicity" so often employed in connection with the subject of Rhythm, means "state of occurring or recurring at fixed intervals of time." Every phenomenal thing manifests periodicity, by reason of the presence and activity of the Principle of Rhythm. Every phenomenal thing has its own rhythmic beat, or mesaure of periodicity. All scientific investigation tends to corroborate the ancient occult axiom: "Everything beats time." A leading scientist has said: "Rhythm is a necessary characteristic of all motion. Given the co-existence everywhere of antagonistic forces—a postulate which is necessitated by our experience—and Rhythm is a necessary corollary. All motion alternates—be it the motion of planets in their orbits, or ethereal corpuscles in their undulations—be it the cadence of speech, or the rise and fall of prices—it became manifest that this perpetual reversal of motion between limits is inevitable."

The atoms in their vibrations manifest Rhythm. The swing of the planets and the whirling of the earth manifest Rhythm. The rise and fall of the tides manifest Rhythm. The swing of the pendulum is interrupted Rhythm. Completed Rhythm is represented only by a completed revolution or circular movement—uninterrupted Rhythm always manifests as a complete movement in an orbit. But inasmuch as the centre between the two extremes is, itself, moving in response to a higher order of Rhythm, we see at last that all completed Rhythm manifests as a

spiral—a circular movement which at the same time
is moving forward.

By the Principle of Rhythm day is followed by
night, and night by day. Summer and winter alternate in their appearance. Sleeping and waking alternate. Work and rest exchange places. Involution is followed by evolution, and evolution by involution. All changes proceed according to rhythmic order and sequence. The conduct of mankind
is regulated by Rhythm. Fashions in dress, in taste,
and in feeling, all come and go, and come again.
Everything ''comes back'' in time. Races rise and
fall, and then rise again, again to fall. The course
of empire wends its way in cyclic procession around
the earth. History repeats itself. Even our emotions have their tidal movements.

A writer has said of an important fact concerning
Rhythm in our emotional states: ''Nothing swings
beyond the limit of its extremes—nothing can pass
beyond its rhythmic limits. Consequently, if a thing
swings far in one direction, it swings back equally
far in the other. Its reaction is in the measure of its
action, though in an opposite direction. If its swing
is great, its extremes are widely apart—if the swing
is small, then the extremes are close together. The
pendulum illustration may be applied to the phenomena on all planes. A short beat of the metronome
allows the rod to move only a short distance each
way—the long beat admits of a wide swing. And,
in the same way, those who suffer keenly also enjoy
keenly, while those whose natures admit of but little
suffering are also incapable of more than a limited
capacity for enjoyment. A pig suffers little, and en-
joys but little; while a highly organized, sensitive
individual suffers the torments of emotional and

mental hell at times, while at others he mounts to the heavenly emotional and mental realms. The pendulum swings as far in one direction as in the other.''

In some of the higher teachings of the Rosicrucians the student is instructed in the application of the Principle of Rhythm to the mastery of his emotional states and feelings. The essence of this secret teaching is that the wise, perceiving the inevitable reaction following action, the ebb tide following the high tide, manage to escape the consequences of the reaction by rising to their higher realms or planes of consciousness just before the time of the backward swing of the emotional pendulum, thus allowing the reactionary movement to be manifested only on their lower planes of consciousness while the Ego dwells serenely on the upper plane.

A writer, speaking along the lines just mentioned, has said: ''The masters taught that by an understanding of the Principle of Rhythm man could escape many bewildering and perplexing changes in his emotional states and feelings. * * * They called this the Process of Neutralization, the operations of which consisted of raising the Ego above the vibrations of the ordinary conscious plane, and on to the higher. This was akin to rising above a thing and allowing the thing to pass beneath one. The occult masters, and their advanced students, polarized themselves at the positive pole of a particular emotional state, and by a process of ''refusing'' or ''denial'' they managed to escape the effects of the swing of the emotional pendulum to the negative pole of that emotion. All individuals who have attained any degree of self-mastery really proceed in this same manner, though usually unconsciously and without a true understanding of the law they are operating. By refusing to allow their negative mental and emotional states to manifest in them, they really 'neutralize' them, and cause them to pass under them on a lower plane of consciousness. The advanced occultist, however, proceeds consciously and deliberately to this end, and acquires a degree of balance, poise, and power almost incredible.''

The further the student penetrates in his investigations, along the lines of the physical, the mental, or the spiritual, the more will he become convinced of the truth of the ancient occult axiom: ''Everything beats time.''

V. The Principles of Cycles

The Principle of Cycles manifests that universal circular direction of process or progress which is apparent in all the manifested world, from its highest to its lowest manifestation. The spirit of this principle was expressed in the ancient occult axiom: ''Everything proceeds in circles.''

It is apparent to all careful thinkers and investigators that all progress or procession of things or events follows the path of the circle. All things, physical, mental, and spiritual manifest the cyclic or circular trend. World and atoms, the Cosmos and man, all are under this law. This principle is understood more clearly when we understand that a completed and uninterrupted manifestation of Rhythm results in the completion of a circular movement— therefore the circular or cyclic trend of things is really closely allied to the Principle of Rhythm, and both Rhythm and Cyclicity are closely allied to the Principle of Vibration.

The following interesting quotation from a writer

on the subject serves to bring out some of the main points concerned in the consideration of the activities of this particular principle:

"Cyclicity is akin to Rhythm, and arise by reason of it. All events tend to move in cyclic trend—in constant circular movement. The Law of Cyclicity manifests in the universal tendency of things to swing in circles. Cyclicity is the outgrowth, or more complex form, of Rhythm. The primal manifestation of Rhythm is action to-and-fro in a straight line or path—a movement backward and forward between two extremes or poles of action. This would be the invariable movement if the particular force manifested were the only manifestation of force or energy in that particular field of the Cosmos. But when the swinging pendulum (free to move in any direction) is subjected to the conflicting attractions and repulsions of other manifestations of force and energy, then there is manifested the universal tendency toward the circular trend—the tendency to convert the straight path of the swing into a circular path or cycle. The action and reaction, the attraction and repulsion, arising from the conflict between the force of the rhythmic swing in a straight line on the one hand, and the attractive and repellant forces from without, on the other hand, tend to swing the moving thing in a perfect circle around a central point, axis, or pivotal centre. And these conflicting forces are in operation through the Cosmos, and the manifestation of Cyclicity may be noticed on all planes. There is ever the evidence of the cyclic trend of things and events—the tendency to move in circles. The electrons in the atoms move in circles, just as do the planets around the sun, and just as does the sun move around some other centre in space.

The highest occult teachings, as well as the highest speculations of science, inform us that there is always a movement in circles around some given point, and the movement of the said point, or centre of motion, around some other centre, and so on, and on, to infinity.''

The same writer continues: ''All events tend to move in cyclic trend—in constant circular movement of continuous recurrence. The experience of man, aided by the reports of history, bears out this statement. The student of human history is struck by the continuous cyclic trend manifested throughout the ages of history. The student of philosophy is attracted by the same evidence in his own field. And so it is with every field of human thought—the cyclic trend is noticeable everywhere. Races and nations rise, flourish, decline, and fall; only to be succeeded by others travelling over the same lines. 'Westward the star of Empire takes its flight'—the centre of political power is constantly changing. The civilizations of Lemuria, Atlantis, Egypt, Chaldea, Rome and Greece arose and passed away. Our own civilization is but travelling over the same general lines. All forms of political government, monarchic, autocratic, democratic, in all their variations, were known in the past as in the present. The same law is observable in the history of philosophical thought. Philosophical theories popular in Greece over two thousand years ago fell into disrepute, but are now again forcing their way to the front. The scientific theories of Causation, Continuity, Determinism, and Evolution were popular in Ancient Greece over two thousand years ago. And they were likewise popular in Ancient Egypt and India centuries before that time. Fashions in literature, dress, and manner constantly recur—travelling 'round and 'round their little circles. Laugh as we may at the absurdity of fashion in dress, nevertheless it is proceeding according to Cyclic Law. Religious ideas are as old as the world—pantheism, polytheism, monotheism, and atheism—all have played their parts of fashion in religious thought, over and over again, and will play them again. The present-day revival of interest in the occult teachings arise from the operations of the same law. And the life of individuals manifest the same trend and tendency. A little thought will convince you that the majority of people travel in circles throughout their entire life. The same old thing, over and over again, recurring at intervals of greater or lesser duration, according to the nature and character of the person. Many people are like the squirrel who travels all day on his whirling wheel—always going but getting nowhere, ever ending just where he began.''

The thoughtful student, considering what has just been called to his attention, will naturally ask us how it is, if this be so, that there is any real progress at all. If, says he, there is nothing but a continuous running around in circles—a constant travelling around without getting anywhere—how is it that there is evident a real progress, a real evolution, a real advancement in the scale of life and being? The answer is simple: given a circular movement around a given point, axis, or centre of attraction, and further given an advancing movement of that centre, point, or axis, it follows that the first circular movement will also be a **spiral** movement. **If the Central Point is advanced, then the circular movement is converted into a spiral movement**—and while there persists a ''going 'round and 'round'' as before, each "going 'round" process travels on a little higher plane, or a more advanced position. And this is just what exists in the Cosmos—a Cosmic Spiral Process, onward and upward, in advancing and rising circles.

An old aphorism of an ancient school of occultism is: "The only escape from Cyclicity is by means of transmutation into Spirality, i. e., by advancing the Central Point of Motion. The conversion of the Circle into the Spiral is one of the highest forms of Alchemy." And in this aphorism is found one of the secrets of Rosicrucianism. The rule operates on each and every plane of being, physical, mental, and spiritual.

A writer has said of this: "The Ego may convert the circle of its life-motion into an advancing and rising spiral, which while carrying him around the life circle will at the same time raise him a stage higher at each turn. The Mountain of Attainment, around which winds the Spiral Path, is travelled only in this way. Around and around the Pilgrims travel, seemingly retracing their steps, but in reality constantly mounting upward. **By advancing the Central Point, by means of the Will,** the wise and the strong convert the Circles into Spirals, and thus advance and attain. This, indeed, as the old aphorism states, 'is one of the highest forms of Mental Alchemy.' "

The further the student penetrates in his investigations, along the lines of the physical, the mental, or the spiritual, the more will he become convinced of the truth of the ancient occult axiom that "Everything proceeds in circles."

VI. The Principle of Polarity

The Principle of Polarity manifests that universal fact of "the pairs of opposites," or "the antinomies," which is apparent in all the manifested world, from its highest to its lowest manifestation. The spirit of this principle was expressed in the ancient occult axiom: "Everything has its Opposite, which is the other pole of its manifestation."

The Principle of Polarity may be stated as follows: "All phenomena manifest polarity, or opposite and contrasted sets of qualities, properties, or powers, operating in opposite and contrasted directions." The ancient philosophers made this one of the chief features of their teachings, under the name of "The Opposites," "The Pairs of Opposites," or "The Antinomies," according to the usage of the respective schools. They held that every phenomenal thing possesses and manifests these pairs of opposite qualities, properties, and powers. They also held that each and every set of polarized opposites constitutes a unity consisting of a reconciliation and balancing of the opposing poles. They also held that every phenomenal thing, itself, is one of a pair of polarized opposites which, together, constitute a greater unity; and so on, either to infinity or until the opposites find final reconciliation and harmony in an Infinite Reality.

The simplest and yet the most characteristic of the many examples and illustrations of Polarity is seen in the presence and activity of the two opposite and contrasting poles of the magnet—the positive and negative poles. The magnet is one—a unity consisting of a balance and a reconciliation of the two opposing poles and their respective activities and powers. The illustration is typical, and fully illustrates the general principle.

We may see evidences of Polarity in any direction toward which we may turn in our search. There is always an up and a down; a top and a bottom; a high and a low; a right and a left; a forward and a backward. There is always a past and a future; a now and a then; a before and an after; a day and a night; a time and an eternity. There is always a fast and a slow; a motion and a rest; a hot and a cold; a good and a bad; a light and a dark; a conscious and an unconscious; an active and an inactive; an involution and an evolution; an analysis and a synthesis; a thesis and an antithesis; a male and a female; a positive and a negative; a youth and an age; a health and a disease; a building-up and a tearing-down; a birth and a death; a coming and a going; a life and a death; material and an immaterial; a heavy and a light; an abstract and a concrete; a long and a short; a broad and a narrow; a large and a small; a north and a south; an east and a west; a love and a hate; a courage and a fear; a faith and a doubt; a belief and a disbelief; a truth and an error; and so on, ad infinitum.

Whenever we see a phenomenal quality, property or characteristic, a state or a condition, we are fully justified in assuming the existence of an opposite to it, which opposite thing will be found to act in the opposite and contrasted direction to it. This is an infallible and invariable rule of phenomenal existence.

In case the opposite of a thing is not known to us, because it has not as yet been discovered by or made known to us, nevertheless in such case we are fully justified in ascribing to the unknown opposite the qualities and characteristics diametrically opposed to the known opposite. The rule is this: "Whatever is affirmed of one of a pair of opposites must be denied to the other"; and whatever is denied to the one, must be affirmed of the other." So true and infallible is this rule that it may be applied and employed as the basis of logical reasoning from the known to the unknown, for the purpose of discovering the latter.

One of the most surprising features of this discovery is that we finally perceive that the two contrasting sets of qualities are really but two aspects or phases of the whole thing—the real thing, or thing in itself—the unity of the two, instead of being two separated and distinct things. Or, stating it in other words, we discover that the two opposing sets of characteristics are merely relative to each other, and together form a correlated unity and balanced whole.

As an illustration of the fact just stated, we may consider the two opposites known as Hot and Cold, respectively; surely there can be no two qualities apparently more distinct and separate from each other—more diametrically different from each other. But careful examination shows us that the two contrasting things are really but degrees, conditions, and states of the same thing. There is no such thing as an "absolute hot," or an "absolute cold." There are merely different degrees of this Hot-Cold pair of opposites, which for convenience we call "Heat." We cannot point out a place on the thermometer where Hot ceases and Cold begins, or vice versa. The two states or conditions blend into each other, and any statement regarding them is found to be merely comparative. If we place one hand in a bowl of very hot water, and the other in a bowl of ice-cold water, and then suddenly withdraw both hands and plunge them into a bowl of lukewarm water, what happens? Simply this, that we find that the hot-water hand feels a sensation of coolness, while the cold-water hand feels a sensation of heat —each experience resulting from the comparison with the previous experience.

We may consider the emotional states of Love and Hate as another illustration of the same principle; surely these two emotions seem irreconcilable and impossible to harmonize. But let us see! At the one end of the emotional scale of Love-Hate we find intense love, then descending on the scale we find varying and gradually lessening degrees of love. Then we find the balanced point of indifference, which seems to be neither love nor hate, but which in reality is the subtle balancing of the two emotions. Then descending the scale we find a faint degree of aversion or dislike; then a series of gradually increasing degrees of dislike, until finally real hate is met with, and so on until we reach the degree of intense and extreme hate. Yet all are seen to be but degrees on the same emotional scale of Love-Hate.

Sometimes there is a rapid change and shift on the scale of the opposites. Love is quickly transmuted to hate; the best friends and most ardent lovers become the bitterest enemies. And, on the other hand, persons who originally detest each other frequently become ardent lovers after a time; and old enemies, when reconciled, frequently become the closest friends. The swing is often as far in one direction as was its former swing in the opposite direction. Up changes to down, as the earth revolves; and hot becomes cold when the vibrations are changed. This also applies to hard and soft, tenuous and solid, etc., the conditions depending entirely upon the rate of vibrations and relative positions of the particles of the matter of which the things are composed. Moreover, constant emphasis or activity of one opposite frequently leads to a manifestation of the other opposite. We often fly to the other extreme of feeling and action, when we have over-emphasized the former emotional states. We get tired and disgusted with one set or condition of things, and feel a desire to fly to the opposite condition or set. Too much of a good thing often causes us to dislike it. Likewise, if we travel far enough west, we finally reach the extreme east, and vice versa. If we travel far enough north, we pass the pole and find ourselves proceeding south. At the North Pole, no matter in what direction we may travel, we always find ourselves travelling south; while at the South Pole, we can travel north only, no matter which way we may step out.

The discovery that "opposites are identical," in the sense of being but the two contrasting poles of the same thing, opens up a wonderful field of mastery to the occultist who has acquainted himself with the law of Polarization, in its phases of Transmutation and Balance.

The understanding of the Principle of Polarity enables the occultist to transmute one mental state into another, along the lines of Polarization. Things belonging to different classes cannot be transmuted into each other, but the opposing poles of the same thing may be so changed—that is, may have a change in their polarity effected and thus be transmuted one into the other. Thus, love can never become east or west, or red or violet; but love may be changed into hate, or hate into love, by a shifting of polarity. Courage may be transmuted into fear, or fear into courage; hard may be changed into soft, dull into sharp, hot into cold, and so on, the transmutation always being between things of the same kind. The fearful man may shift his polarity and by thus changing his emotional vibrations may become filled with courage. Likewise, the slothful man may shift his polarity into activity and energetic action. The key lies in the fact that in this process of transmutation there is not an actual change of one thing into another distinct thing, but rather a shifting of the centre of polar force from one extreme of the scale to the other, just as one would shift the carriage of his typewriter from 1 to 70, or change the focus of an opera glass.

A writer on the subject has said of this particular point: ''In addition to the changing of one's own mental states by the operation of the art of Polarization, the principle may be extended so as to embrace the phenomena of the influence of one mind over that of another, of which so much has been written and taught of late years. When it is understood that Mental Induction is possible, that is that mental states may be produced by 'induction' from those of other persons, then we can see how readily a certain rate of mental vibrations, or polarization of a certain mental state, may be communicated from one person to another, and the polarity of the second person be changed accordingly. It is along these lines that many excellent results of 'mental treatment' are obtained, though the practitioner may not understand the nature of the principle he is using. For instance, a person is 'blue,' melancholy, depressed in spirits, and full of fear. A mental scientist bringing his own mind up to the desired vibration, by means of his own will which thus produces the desired polarization in his own case, then by induction communicates these polarized vibrations to the mind of the patient, the result being that the patient's emotional states are converted from the negative polarization to the positive. A knowledge of the existence of this great occult principle will enable the occultist to better understand his own mental states, and those of other people. He will see that these states are all matters of degree, and seeing thus he will be able to raise or lower his mental and emotional vibrations at will—to change his mental poles, and thus be a master of his emotions instead of being a slave to them. And by his knowledge he will be able to aid his fellow men intelligently, and by appropriate methods change their mental and emotional polarization when the same is desirable.''

In concluding our consideration of the Principle of Polarity, we ask the student to study carefully the following words written by one who has a knowledge of the great subject of Balance, the art of which consists in finding the Centre between the Two Extremes, and thus maintaining a Poise and Balance which is undisturbed by any mental or emotional storm. This writer says:

''Poise is Power. Poise results from Balance. Balance is secured by adjusting and maintaining the Centre between the Poles of the Pairs of Opposites. By Balanced Poise the Master neutralizes Polarity and Rhythm, by resolving them into Unity. In the Heart of the Storm is Peace. In the Centre of Life there is Poise and Power. Seek it ever, O Neophyte —for in it thou shalt find thyself. The foregoing sentences compose the substance of an ancient arcane aphorism, in which is contained the seed thought generated in the centuries of thought and experience of the arcane teachers. Do not pass it by because of its simplicity. Poised balance is the aim and goal of the arcane initiates. It is the secret of mastery. There is always a centre of everything. But the centre exists only because of the existence of the circumference. There is always a point or poise between the poles of every pair of opposites. But that point exists only because the extremes exist. And in the central point is always found the power of the whole event or thing. In the centre of gravity of the earth one would be able to remain in a position of perfect poise, unsupported except by the concentrated gravity of the whole earth. So nicely poised that a mere effort of the will would exert sufficient energy to propel him in any desired direction. The power of the opposites are concentrated at the central point. There all power is to be found, and there only. The axiom 'Action and Reaction are equal' indicates a central point in which lies the true lever which will move the whole. At the centre one is able to use action and reaction without being subject to either. The initiate strives to attain the state of equilibrium and absolute poise. He yearns to master the art of traversing the razor-edge of Life, balancing himself perfectly, like the trained mental athlete that he is, by means of the balancing-pole of the Opposites which he has firmly grasped. Pitting the Opposites one against the other—balancing law by law—the Master traverses the slender tightrope thread which separates the world of desire from the world of will. O Neophyte, in the Centre of Life shalt thou indeed find Poise and Power. In the Heart of the Storm shalt thou find Peace. In the Centre of the Cosmos shalt thou find THYSELF. He who finds the Centre of Himself, finds the Centre of the Cosmos. For, at the last, they are ONE!"

The student when confronted with questions and problems in which a choice is difficult by reason of the strong activity of both extremes of polarization— of both of the Pair of Opposites, is advised to seek out the Centre between the two opposing poles, and to stand firmly there, feeling assured that there, and there only is the place of peace, poise and power. In the one word "BALANCE" there is to be found the Secret of many, or most of the perplexing questions of Life. Seek ever, Poise and Balance, and you will have Power and Peace!

The further the student penetrates in his investigations along the lines of the physical, the mental, and the spiritual, the more will he become convinced of the truth of the ancient occult axiom that "Everything has its Opposite, which is the other pole of its manifestation."

VII. The Principle of Sex

The Principle of Sex manifests in the universal presence of sex distinction and activity which is apparent in all the manifested world, from its highest to its lowest manifestations. The spirit of this principle was expressed in the ancient occult axiom: "Sex is omnipresent and all-pervasive in the universe. All creation is generation, and all generation proceeds from Sex."

All deep students of occultism, and many students of modern science, perceive the truth of the Rosicrucian ancient doctrine that Sex is all-pervasive, all-present, and is the cause of all creation, for creation always results from generation, and generation proceeds from sex-activity. There is Sex manifested in everything—the masculine and feminine principles are ever at work in the universe. This not only on the physical plane of being, but also on the mental and spiritual planes of being. On the physical plane Sex manifests physical generation; on the mental plane it manifests mental generation; and on the spiritual plane it manifests spiritual generation. An understanding of the Cosmic Principle of Sex will give one a clear insight into many subjects which have proved perplexing to the majority of thinkers.

In a preceding chapter of this book we have called your attention to the fact that the activities of the electrons, the atoms, and the corpuscles of which matter is composed, are purely sexual activities— that all attraction is sex-attraction, and that as all Cosmic activity results from Attraction, therefore Sex is the Motive Power behind the activities of the Cosmos. A careful examination of the discoveries of modern science which are being announced from year to year will convince the student that all are explainable under the Rosicrucian theory of the Principle of Sex, and are explainable under no other hypothesis.

Passing on to the Plane of Mind, we find that many of the discoveries of modern psychology tend to verify the Rosicrucian theory also. Modern psychologists are devoting much time and space to their presentations of the various theories and discussions of that "other mind" which they variously call the "subjective mind," the "subconscious mind," the "subliminal mind," etc., etc. In all of their theories, however, one point stands out prominently, i. e., the point that this "other mind" is subject to stimulating influences from the "conscious" or "objective" mind, and after being so subjected to the influence of stimulus of the latter the "other mind" becomes fertile and produces a wealth of ideas, thoughts, and actions. But so far none of the psychologists have even attempted to explain the nature of the influence or stimulus of the one mind upon the other. And here is where the Rosicrucian teachings are much needed, for the Rosicrucian recognizes and realizes at once the fact that the "other mind" is **feminine,** and the stimulating mind is **masculine,** and that the process is clearly one of fertilization followed by mental conception and generation.

So clear is the analogy that one has but to have his attention directed toward it to realize its truth and its proper application to the case before us. It is so clear that one, on learning it, cannot see why the promulgators of the "dual-mind" theories, and their commentators, can have failed to perceive the secret underlying the phenomena discovered by them and embodied in their various theories. Thompson J. Hudson, in his book "The Law of Psychic Phenomena," in which in 1893 he announced his celebrated theory of "the dual mind," came near to perceiving the secret hidden in the teaching of the ancient occultists, but his prejudices caused him to pass it by. In his statement, at the beginning of his second chapter of said book, he says: "The mystic jargon of the Hermetic philosophers discloses the same general idea," i. e., the general idea of the duality of mind, but he failed to follow up the promising lead, and thus lost the opportunity to complete his discovery—or rediscovery, for the duality of the mind's activities has been known to occultists for ages.

The "other mind" of the human individual may be regarded as a mental womb—in fact the ancients so styled it—in which is generated a wealth of mental offspring. It is a mine of latent possibilities of generation—the generation of mental progeny of all sorts and kinds. Its powers of mental generative energy are enormous. But it does not generate except under the stimulus of the "conscious mind" of its owner, or some other individual. The phenomena of Suggestion and Hypnotism are explainable under the Rosicrucian Theory of Mental Sex. A writer on this subject has said:

"Suggestion and Hypnotism operate in the same way, viz., by the Masculine Principle projecting its vibrations toward the Feminine Principle in the mind of the other person, the latter taking the seed-thought and allowing it to develop into maturity when it is born on the plane of consciousness. The Masculine Principle in the mind of the person giving the suggestion directs a vibratory current toward the Feminine Principle in the mind of the person who is the object of the suggestions, and the latter accepts it according to natural laws, unless the will interposes an objection. The seed-thought thus lodged in the mind of the other person grows and develops and in time is regarded as the rightful mental offspring of the person, whereas it is really like the cuckoo's egg placed in the nest of the sparrow; and like the offspring of the cuckoo, it destroys the rightful offspring of the owner of the nest. The proper method is for the Masculine and Feminine Principles in the mind of a person to co-ordinate and to act harmoniously in conjunction with each other. But unfortunately the Masculine Principle in the mind of the average person is too lazy to act—the activities of the Will too slight—the consequence being that such persons are ruled almost entirely by the minds and wills of other persons, whom they allow to do their thinking and willing for them. The majority of persons are but mere shadows and echoes of other persons having stronger wills and minds than themselves. The strong men and women of the world invariably manifest the Masculine Principle of Will, and their strength depends materially upon this fact. Instead of living by the impressions made upon their minds by others, they dominate their own minds by means of their own will, obtaining the kind of thoughts desired; and moreover they dominate the minds of others, likewise, in the same manner. Look at the strong people, see how they manage to implant their seed-thoughts in the minds of the masses of the people, thus causing the latter to think thoughts in accordance with the desires and wills of the strong individuals. This is why the masses of the people are such sheeplike creatures, never originating an idea of their own, nor using their own powers of mental activity. The manifestation of Mental Sex may be noticed all around us in our daily life. The magnetic persons are those who are able to use the Masculine Mental Principle in the direction of impressing their ideas upon others. The actor who makes people weep or cry as he wills is employing this principle, more or less unconsciously. So is the successful orator, statesman, preacher, writer, or other person who is before the public. The peculiar influence exerted by some persons over others is explainable in this way—

the operation of Mental Sex activity in the form of vibratory mental currents. Here we may find the secret of personal magnetism, personal influence, fascination, etc.''

The Principle of Sex manifests and operates also on the Spiritual Plane of being, according to its characteristic principles, and its results are spiritual generation and regeneration. We regret that we are not permitted to go deeply into this phase of the subject in this book, but a detailed consideration of the operation of Sex on this high plane would be contrary to the interests of the best in occultism, and would invite a misuse of power on the part of unprincipled persons who fail to understand the evil consequences to themselves coming as a reaction following actions of this kind. The true student, however, by using his power of reasoning by analogy, doubtless will be able to work out some of the problems concerned with the phase of the question thus mentioned. Such will find the secret in the old axiom: ''As above, so below; as below, so above.''

The further the student penetrates in his investigations along the lines of the physical, the mental, and the spiritual, the more will he become convinced of the truth of the ancient occult axiom that ''Sex is omnipresent and all-pervasive in the universe. All creation is generation, and all generation proceeds from Sex.''

FINIS

3

5

4